DAY STARTERS FOR STUDENTS

60 DEVOTIONAL THOUGHTS TO STAY HONEST WITH GOD

Greg Johnson

FaithHappenings Publishers

Copyright © 2016 by Greg Johnson.

All rights reserved. No part of this publication may be reproduced, distributed or transmitted in any form or by any means, electronic or mechanical, including photocopying, recording, or by any information storage and retrieval system, without permission in writing from the copyright owner.

FaithHappenings Publishers
7061 S. University Blvd., Suite 307
Centennial, CO 80122

Scripture quotations are from The Holy Bible, English Standard Version® (ESV®), copyright © 2001 by Crossway, a publishing ministry of Good News Publishers. Used by permission. All rights reserved.

Cover Design: ©Angela Bouma
Book Layout ©2013 BookDesignTemplates.com

Day Starters for Students © Greg Johnson

ISBN: Softcover: 978-1-941555-08-8

This book was printed in the United States of America.

To order additional copies of this book, contact:
info@faithhappenings.com

FaithHappenings Publishers,
a division of FaithHappenings.com

Stuff in this Book

Getting Behind the Wheel of Life 1

1. Where're You Walkin', Standin', and Sittin'? 3
2. Half Full or Half Empty? 6
3. Life—The Ultimate Roller Coaster! 9
4. King of the Hill 12
5. Just One Thing 15
6. Slow Poison 19
7. Starting at the End of the Book 22
8. The Best Part of Waking Up 26
9. Aiming for the Target 29
10. Coming Full Circle 32
11. Consider 36
12. The Joy of Possessing Nothing 38
13. These Opposites Don't Attract 41
14. The Classroom of Life 44
15. Taking It Personally 46
16. He Knows Exactly 50
17. Where Heart and Tongue Meet 53
18. "Could You Have a Bad Memory, Please?" 56
19. Keep Your Reputation Strong 59
20. Embracing Both Inevitables 62

21. "Hit Me With Your Best Shot" 65
22. What Type of Drowner Are You? 68
23. Angels on Assignment 71
24. The Human Disease and Dis-ease 74
25. "If You're Going to Break Something . . ." 78
26. He Always Answers 81
27. Waiting for Justice 84
28. The Invited Ruler 87
29. Making the Grade 90
30. The Only Sure Thing 93
31. He'll Never Leave 96
32. Free Road Maps, Anyone? 98
33. Casting Worries Aside 101
34. What's Your Rep? 104
35. What Are You Afraid Of? 107
36. The Patient Heart Changer 110
37. Bridge Builder 113
38. The Evil Called Good 116
39. Once You've Truly Known Him 119
40. A Miraculous Mystery 122
41. The Applause of Heaven 125
42. The Unavoidable Subject 129
43. Waiting for Deliverance 132
44. Conditional Promises 135
45. Moving to the Next Level 138

46. The Loneliness Solution	141
47. Does God Make Mistakes in Judgment?	145
48. Looking Through the Right End of the Telescope	148
49. More than Words	151
50. The Freedom to Go	154
51. Under Control	157
52. A Heart Undivided	160
53. He's God, and You're Not	163
54. Clean Slate Freedom	166
55. Blessed Discipline	169
56. True Beauty	173
57. The Not-So-Great Pretender	176
58. The Sin of Divination	180
59. The Hugest Calling of All	183
60. Off the Chart	186
Wrap Up	189

Getting Behind the Wheel of Life

For most students, getting behind the wheel of life—and the Christian life—seems pretty easy. Sure, there have been a few unexpected turns and potholes along the way, but most students have yet to encounter the BIG STUFF in the road.

The BIG STUFF, however, IS coming.

Flat tires. Icy roads. Traffic jams. Fog. Engine trouble. A big moose in the middle of a small back road. You *will* have driving mishaps, some caused by others, some by you. You won't be able to avoid all hazards. (OK, maybe the moose.)

And since you're alive, you won't be able to avoid many of life's hazards, either. The road ahead is filled with them. Some are way off in the distance, but a few are just around the next turn.

My goal in writing this book is to clue you in on what's ahead and to give you some knowledge and a few skills necessary to handle what you run into . . . or what runs into you!

Just living life will teach you a lot, but if you can learn from someone else's experience—mine, your parents or grandparents, teachers and coaches—you'll be able to deal with your problems much more easily.

What's included here are sixty short passages from the Psalms (one per day, of course), a brief devotional, a few questions, two follow-up scriptures, and a summary makes each "thought" short and sweet.

I chose the Psalms as a springboard for discussion because that book contains some of the most profound portions of God's Word. The Psalms are emotional, honest, poetic, and deep.

You'll notice two themes as you read: (1) your choices and (2) God's choices.

YOUR CHOICES. Just as being a safe driver requires you to make the right moment-by-moment decisions, living life in ways that benefits your soul also requires you to make the correct choices. The hazards are many, and the consequences for making the wrong choices are potentially disastrous.

GOD'S CHOICES. You may never before have considered the choices God has made through the centuries: He's chosen to love you, to die for you, and to be there for you when you need him. But amazingly, God has ultimately *chosen* to let you make the biggest choice of all: Will you let Him take control of the wheel of your life . . . or not?

I hope this book helps you be more honest with yourself about the choices you have made and are going to make. Most of all, I hope it deepens your appreciation for the choices God has made on your behalf.

ONE

Where're You Walkin', Standin', and Sittin'?

*Blessed is the man who does not walk
in the counsel of the wicked or stand in
the way of sinners or sit in the seat of mockers.*
Psalms 1:1

God could have launched the book of Psalms with any of hundreds of different topics, but He chose to talk about our choice of friends. The reason: While you'll be influenced greatly by your parents, teachers, and a few others, no one will influence you more than your friends.

In middle school, Gary spent time with his friends from church who loved sports. It didn't matter what season it was—or the weather—they were outside throwing, catching, shooting, or hitting some kind of ball. When high school arrived, the athletic ability he'd developed with his friends allowed him to make varsity in football and baseball. But while his physical coordination brought him new friends on the field, his lack of social coordination kept him from the cute girls, something he was now much more interested in pursuing. The problem, he discovered, was his old friends weren't in the "cool group." So he chose to quit spending time with his buddies from middle school. The results were predictable: parties, "recreational" drinking, a few "harmless" drugs, temptations with girls, no desire for church . . . Soon Gary was a changed man.

The people you choose to invest your hundreds of hours of free time with not only determine present behavior, but they could determine your eternal destiny. If your friends have no desire to explore a genuine faith in Christ, or don't care about giving attention to their spiritual needs, *you'll* be tempted to neglect your needs, as well.

Does that mean you can only hang out with those who are perfect? Examining the opening verse gives the answer. The psalmist is warning us about being friends with the wicked. He isn't saying not to speak with those who are wicked. He's counseling us not to spend a lot of time with them. He also warns us about spending time with sinners and mockers.

Sinners, of course, is a word that applies to everyone. But in this verse it means those who consistently try to control their own lives, separate from God's influence. *Mockers* are those who put down authority and anything that doesn't validate their lifestyle.

Think about all of the friends you have. Are you following the advice in this verse? God cares who you spend time with. He knows the joys of having close friends who help to take you in the right direction, and He realizes the hazards of spending your time with those who do not have a mind for God. So should you.

MORE REFLECTION:
- "Do not be misled: 'Bad company corrupts good character'" (1 Corinthians 15:33).

- "Do not be yoked together with unbelievers. For what do righteousness and wickedness have in common? Or what fellowship can light have with darkness?" (2 Corinthians 6:14).
- "Away from me, you evildoers, that I may keep the commands of my God!" (Psalms 119:115).

FOR PONDERING FURTHER:

1. How do you know who's OK to hang around with and who isn't?
2. Should a parent ever have any say-so in who you choose for friends?
3. What should your parents do if your behavior starts to change negatively because you're hanging out with certain friends?
4. Think about your friends. Do they encourage you to love and follow God? If not, what should you do?

LAST THOUGHT:

CHOOSE YOUR FRIENDS WISELY.

TWO

Half Full or Half Empty?

*This is the day the Lord has made;
let us rejoice and be glad in it.*
Psalms 118:24

How do you respond when your feet first hit the floor to start the day? Is it "Good morning, Lord!" or "Good Lord, morning"?

No, not everyone can be a morning person. And if you share a bedroom with someone who is . . . well, it's not always a pretty picture. But beyond your wake-up habits, you are faced with several immediate choices each time you wipe the sleep out of your eyes and prepare yourself for another day.

1. Will I recognize God is with me, or will I mentally leave Him at home?

2. Will I attack the challenges of the day or dread facing anything that puts a wrinkle in my plans?

3. Will I view the day as filled with opportunity or will I treat it as another miserable day of existence?

The basic choice you have is whether to be *optimistic* or *pessimistic* about the day God has given you.

The optimists say yes to the first half of each of the questions above. They know they only get one chance to enjoy life moment by moment, that once time ticks by, those seconds can never be reclaimed. So they choose to view life from a more positive angle. The glass is half full, not half empty!

In case you're wondering, optimists aren't people whose lives are void of troubles. They have as many as anyone else. But they've learned to keep things in perspective. If they break an arm, they're glad they didn't break both of them—and one of their legs, as well. If they don't play much for the team, they notice the kids who didn't make it at all (or see the girl in the wheelchair at school), and are thankful they had the chance to even try out. If they didn't get the iPhone they wanted for Christmas, they take a look around their room and around the house and notice all the stuff they *do* have.

The pessimists have trouble too, but their responses are different. Since the glass is always half empty, they look for the negative aspect about everything—then let those around them know about it.

Was Jesus a pessimist or an optimist? How did he respond when he faced a tough situation?

"Master, there are 5,000 men here," a disciple asked. "How are we going to feed them?" Did Jesus respond, "I hope we can find an ant hill for all these sluggards to feast on"? No, he found a solution.

How does God respond, for example, when He looks at a girl whose heart is rebellious?

Does He say, "Her heart is so wicked, she's really not worth dying for. But if I have to . . ."?

Not even close.

He sees the potential for good and is fully confident that if she knew the truth, she could eventually respond to it and turn her life around. To Him—as it relates to His special and unique creation—the glass is ALWAYS half full.

If you're not the optimistic type, what will it take for you to look at life more positively? What will it take for you to say each morning, "This is the day the Lord has made, I will rejoice and be glad in it"?

MORE REFLECTION:

- "Be joyful always" (1 Thessalonians 5:16).
- "Blessed are you when people insult you, persecute you and falsely say all kinds of evil against you because of me. Rejoice and be glad, because great is your reward in heaven, for in the same way they persecuted the prophets who were before you" (Matthew 5:11-12).

FOR PONDERING FURTHER:

1. Are you a pessimist or an optimist?
2. Why might it be important to look at life the way God would?
3. Name one thing you could do to become more optimistic.
4. Talk with your parents about how they could encourage you to become more optimistic.

LAST THOUGHT:

TRY TO SEE EACH DAY AND EVERY CIRCUMSTANCE THE WAY GOD WOULD.

THREE

Life—The Ultimate Roller Coaster!

Why, O Lord, do you stand far off?
Why do you hide yourself in times
of trouble?
Psalms 10:1

One minute the psalmist is waxing poetic about God's faithfulness and power... and the next he's screaming questions about whether God is playing hide-and-seek. Does the guy have two personalities that never talk to each other?

Or is he... normal?

King David (yes, the Goliath-killer) wasn't schizophrenic or a loony-toon candidate. He was normal. In case you haven't noticed, life is something of a roller coaster ride. It has ups and downs and twists and turns. Sometimes it's exhilarating... other times it makes you throw up. It's life!

Well, David's life had tons of ups and downs. And occasionally, he didn't mind asking ridiculous questions he already knew the answer to. But the questions weren't really ridiculous, were they? They were honest. That's why God left them in the Bible. He likes honesty. He was trying to let you know that it's OK to get angry once in a while—even at Him. He understands about life and the difficulties it presents, and He knows it'll make you ticked once in a while.

Have you ever...

- been dumped by a boyfriend or girlfriend?
- heard your parents yell and scream at each other till it hurt so bad inside you were sick to your stomach?
- studied really hard for a test, only to get a failing grade?
- been misunderstood and neglected by someone you thought was a friend?

Welcome to life on planet Earth!

So what do you do when life makes you lose your lunch? In this passage, and dozens of others, you get the clue that God doesn't mind honest emotion. It's OK to question Him, get mad at Him, and accuse Him of causing something He didn't really cause.

But when you're done venting, don't forget to hang around long enough to see who cleans up the mess. Don't forget about the one who cleaned up the ultimate mess—our sin—for eternity.

MORE REFLECTION:

- "And at the ninth hour Jesus cried out in a loud voice, 'Eloi, Eloi, lama sabachtani?' which means, 'My God, my God, why have you forsaken me?'" (Mark 15:34—See, even Jesus felt forsaken.)
- "Lord, who may dwell in your sanctuary? Who may live on your holy hill? He whose walk is blameless and who does what is righteous, who speaks the truth from his heart" (Psalms 15:1-2—God values truth from the heart!)

FOR PONDERING FURTHER:

1. When have you felt as if God has hidden Himself from you?
2. Have you ever expressed to God your anger or disappointment with Him?
3. Is God ever really standing far off or hiding from you?
4. Talk with your parent about how you feel about being so honest with God.

LAST THOUGHT:

KNOW THAT GOD CAN TAKE ANY QUESTIONS YOU THROW HIS WAY.

FOUR

King of the Hill

*I have installed my King on Zion,
my holy hill.*
Psalms 2:6

In Old Testament times the people of God had an earthy king they could look to for government and spiritual direction. His place of kingship was Mt. Zion, more commonly known as Jerusalem. The king and the city were constant, visible reminders of who was in charge.

Today, however, Christians don't have that visible reminder. Instead, we have a king who takes his throne someplace hidden—our hearts. And because his seat of honor is invisible, sometimes you might forget he's there. In fact, it's your natural bent to replace your unseen king with something (or someone) you're much more acquainted with—YOURSELF!

Your heart is God's "holy hill." He wants to be king of this hill because He knows that only under his leadership will your life be led in the right direction. Plus, there's a supernatural security that occurs when you're able to keep him on the throne of your heart. But in order to experience that security—and be confident in his leadership—you must "install" him. It's your choice.

When you install a new stereo in your car, you have to purchase it then move it from the store to underneath your dash. It's a choice . . . and a bit of work.

When you ask Jesus Christ into your heart and receive his free gift of salvation, you have, in essence, made a choice to install this supernatural king on the throne of your life. While this is a one-time choice, it's also a daily choice. As each day dawns, you have the power to place yourself or *God* on the throne of your life. That's why it's wise to pray each morning, *"Lord, today, I install you as King of my life. Keep my pride and desires far from that throne so that I may follow your leadership closely."*

MORE REFLECTION:

- "I pray that out of his glorious riches he may strengthen you with power through his Spirit in your inner being, so that Christ may dwell in your hearts through faith" (Ephesians 3:16-17a).
- "I have been crucified with Christ and I no longer live, but Christ lives in me. The life I live in the body, I live by faith in the Son of God, who loved me and gave himself for me" (Galatians 2:20).

FOR PONDERING FURTHER:

1. Name three things you can install.
2. How would installing these things be a choice?
3. Do you think people in the Old Testament had it easier than you because they had an earthly king to look to for spiritual guidance?

4. What is most difficult about following an invisible king like Jesus Christ?

LAST THOUGHT:
MAKING THE CHOICE TO INSTALL JESUS ON THE THRONE OF YOUR LIFE IS SOMETHING THAT MUST HAPPEN EVERY DAY.

FIVE

Just One Thing . . .

> *One thing I ask of the Lord, this is what I seek:*
> *that I may dwell in the house of the Lord all*
> *the days of my life, to gaze upon the beauty*
> *of the Lord and to seek him in his temple.*
> Psalms 27:4

If you read this verse again, you'll notice that David didn't want just ONE thing; he wanted three. He wanted to:
- Dwell in the house of the Lord forever
- Gaze upon God's beauty
- Seek God in his temple

As I read this verse, I thought about the opposite of each of the three things David was requesting. It helped put the prayer in perspective.

Dwelling in the house of the Lord is far different than roaming in the realm of Satan. There is a permanence and security to being in the Lord's house, whereas there's restlessness and discontentment around the kingdom of darkness. If heaven is perfect peace, hell is eternity without peace. If heaven's reward is living without fear, hell's punishment is to wander aimlessly in a place with no joy or hope.

Can you imagine never being at peace . . . for eternity?

To gaze upon God's beauty may sound boring, but I suspect that David realized God must be infinitely more beautiful than any person or thing in creation. But just as beauty can stop you in your tracks, causing you to stare in wonder, true ugliness can cause you to look away in nausea.

Can you imagine living in a place where you never wanted to look up because everything you saw made you sick to your stomach . . . for eternity?

Do you know what it's like to want to—really badly—talk to someone? You have news that you can't wait to get out. The words almost burst from within you when you finally get close to that person. That's the way it will be for us in heaven. We will want to seek out God's presence so much that we won't be able to contain ourselves.

But if you have ever known that feeling of "I can't wait to see them," you've probably also experienced the dread of carrying inside the feeling of "I just can't BEAR to see them!"

When you do everything you can to avoid someone—a friend, parent, teacher, or coach—your heart aches and your insides churn with fear of having to look that person in the eye.

Can you imagine living in a place where you always lived in dread of seeing someone you didn't want to see . . . for eternity?

Sometimes God allows a person a great and terrible gift. He'll allow them to picture what life would be like totally separated from Him for eternity. Perhaps that is what happened to David before he wrote this psalm.

True strength and assurance is found not simply in a place called heaven, but in the beauty you will see and the feeling you will possess at wanting to spend eternity with the one who gave His all to keep you from a place of terrifying darkness.

MORE REFLECTION:

- "But our citizenship is in heaven. And we eagerly await a Savior from there, the Lord Jesus Christ, who, by the power that enables him to bring everything under his control, will transform our lowly bodies so that they will be like his glorious body" (Philippians 3:20-21).
- "Now we know that if the earthly tent we live in is destroyed, we have a building from God, an eternal house in heaven, not built by human hands. Meanwhile we groan, longing to be clothed with our heavenly dwelling, because when we are clothed, we will not be found naked. For while we are in this tent, we groan and are burdened, because we do not wish to be unclothed but to be clothed with our heavenly dwelling, so that what is mortal may be swallowed up by life. Now it is God who has made us for this very purpose and has given us the Spirit as a deposit, guaranteeing what is to come" (2 Corinthians 5:1-5).

FOR PONDERING FURTHER:

1. If you were to ask God for one thing, what would it be?
2. Why do you think the things David sought after were so important to him?
3. What do you think heaven will be like?
4. How about hell?

LAST THOUGHT:
LOOKING FORWARD TO AN ETERNITY IN GOD'S PRESENCE MIGHT BE WORTH THINKING ABOUT MORE OFTEN.

SIX

Slow Poison

I will set before my eyes no vile thing.
The deeds of faithless men I hate;
they will not cling to me.
Psalms 101:3

There's a lot of crud to gaze at these days. Many "adult" websites, movies, and online videos are easily accessible. And none of it comes even close to representing God's ideal about sex and relationships.

It's been said that the eyes are the window to the soul. Through them you allow all of the images in the world to enter your mind, filter down to your heart, and permeate your entire being.

Your eyes are also a technical wonder. Through them you're able to marvel at the beauties of God's creation, taking in a snapshot that can move you to thanksgiving and praise. But beauty isn't the only thing that can move you. Suffering can, as well. It can impress upon you to feel what Jesus felt for the poor and destitute: compassion. Your heart is often forced into action by what you see, and another human being is helped along in his journey.

But your eyes can also see the profane. The raunchy, if you will. Sadly, images of the human body being misused and mistreated are all around. The "adult" garbage is obvious, but even TV sitcoms, "viewer discretion" dramas, the internet, and cable can all show an endless parade of skin. These media—the electronic boxes that carry the images, the slick paper—aren't evil. It's the images themselves that are destructive. Yet we know those same pictures that are nauseating to some are also enticing to others. Regretfully, they are here to stay. These images are a tempting, alluring, slow-acting poison to the spirit.

Therefore, Christians who desire to live a life that reflects God's purity have tough choices to make.

Daily choices.

Hourly choices that are only a mouse click away.

Since the prospect of not brushing up against the profane portions of the media are slim, the Christian who wants to maintain higher levels of purity in obedience to Christ must be constantly on the alert. In the truest sense of the word, the believer is in a war. And your enemy is patient. He understands that the best strategy to defeat you is to slowly and stealthily infiltrate the soul with poisonous images.

You'll find that it is the small, compromising choices of what you set before your eyes that will steal your faith, not the "big" mistakes. The enemy is currently waging war for your soul, and battles must be won. Each time you turn away and turn it off, you win another battle.

MORE REFLECTION:

- "Finally, brothers, whatever is true, whatever is noble, whatever is right, whatever is pure, whatever is lovely, whatever is admirable—if anything is excellent or praiseworthy—think about such things" (Philippians 4:8).

- "Since, then, you have been raised with Christ, set your hearts on things above, where Christ is seated at the right hand of God. Set your minds on things above, not on earthly things. For you died, and your life is now hidden with Christ in God" (Colossians 3:1-3).

FOR PONDERING FURTHER:

1. What are some media with vile images that are easy for you to avoid?
2. Are there any that are tougher to stay away from?
3. What steps can you take to avoid these images?
4. How have people you know been affected by taking in images that are not of God?

LAST THOUGHT:

DO ALL YOU CAN TO CHOOSE TO SET NO WORTHLESS OR VILE THING BEFORE YOUR EYES.

SEVEN

Starting at the End of the Book

*Show me, O Lord, my life's end
and the number of my days; let me
know how fleeting is my life.*
Psalms 39:4

The verse above is an odd prayer for a king to pray, don't you think? Shouldn't he have simply prayed for a long life, lots of possessions, his enemies to be defeated, and his children to do well? Though he probably prayed for those things, on this day he was prompted to pray for something few of us would consider: What can I learn about life by reading from the end of the book?

David wasn't asking for a glimpse into how many wrinkles he would have, what his bank account balance would look like, or how good his eyesight would be. He wanted to discover life's most important priorities before it was too late to enjoy them.

He knew, as most of us do, that our days are hectic. Multi-leveled and multi-faceted priorities selfishly crowd out the deeper, more cherished, simple pleasures of living. But death, or at least the gentle whisper of death, has a way of pushing your internal buttons in a way you can't ignore. Suddenly, what seemed so important yesterday is barely retrieved from the memory banks today. Life is quickly boiled down to what truly is essential.

What do you think David saw in response to his prayer? What do you think he realized was important in life? Let's imagine his last few words:

1. *"At the end of life, it's my closeness with God that means the most."* The heart must get humble awfully quickly when there are but moments between this life and the next. Only the foolish and stubbornly proud would hold onto their pride when they are close to gazing upon the face of their maker.

2. *"My family has been the greatest earthly gift of all."* When the last few days are recognized, important last words are said, and petty grievances and hurts are immediately forgotten. Expressions of love are handed out with a genuineness no one could mistake. It is a rare person who would want to die with unforgiveness in his heart or who would hold tightly to the power to forgive another. Cleaning up—and keeping clean—family relationships should always be a priority.

3. *"For my dear friends, I am truly thankful."* Again, words are spoken, handshakes and hugs are given, and slates are wiped clean.

While there might be some LAST THOUGHT:s on the disposition of property, conspicuously absent would be any mention of achievements, possessions, certificates, or trophies. All of the periphery in life is vaporized into a few simple common denominators: God, family, and friends.

Though you may not think about it often, you know your end. This marvelous prayer of David is a picture God has lovingly painted for you. He has brush-stroked a truth in this one sentence that the perceptive immediately grasp. The priorities that make life worth living are not work, pleasure, or accumulated "toys," but God, family, and friends.

How do your priorities stack up?

MORE REFLECTION:

- "... their hearts were not loyal to him, they were not faithful to his covenant. Yet he was merciful; he forgave their iniquities and did not destroy them. Time after time he restrained his anger and did not stir up his full wrath. He remembered that they were but flesh, a passing breeze that does not return" (Psalms 78:37-39).
- "As a father has compassion on his children, so the Lord has compassion on those who fear him; for he knows how we are formed, he remembers that we are dust. As for man, his days are like grass, he flourishes like a flower of the field; the wind blows over it and it is gone, and its place remembers it no more. But from everlasting to everlasting the Lord's love is with those who fear him, and his righteousness with their children's children—with those who keep his covenant and remember to obey his precepts" (Psalms 103:13-18).

FOR PONDERING FURTHER:

1. How would your priorities change if you found out you only had a year to live?
2. How about a week?

3. How do your current priorities stack up against the ones you'd have in the first two questions?

LAST THOUGHT:
LIVING AS THOUGH YOU WILL MEET YOUR END TOMORROW MAY BE THE BEST WAY TO LIVE TODAY.

EIGHT

The Best Part of Waking Up

*In the morning, O Lord, you hear my
voice; in the morning I lay my requests
before you and wait in expectation.*
Psalms 5:3

Busy. Hectic. Fast-paced. Most of us live life on the edge. Our priority lists are full, and the time to pursue a quiet time with the Savior often gets pushed aside. Between school, homework, a job, sports, and other extracurricular activities, finding five or ten minutes a day to spend with God is becoming a lost art, a forgotten discipline.

In biblical times, of course, people weren't tied to the clock, to school bus schedules and deadlines. So they had hours to do nothing but think and meditate and read their Bibles, right? No, that wasn't the case. Without the help of modern conveniences, daily life was much more consuming for them. They had to gather each day's food. Someone had to get a fire going so the morning meal could be prepared. Since they couldn't turn on tap water, someone had to walk—often a mile or more—to fetch it for cooking and cleaning. As soon as the sun rose they were busy trying to provide food and shelter for themselves. All of these essential tasks took time—daylight time. And because there were no lightbulbs they had to hustle to get all of their chores done before the sun went down.

Whether or not you're a morning person, it's best to take a few minutes to spend with God before the day gets rolling. Try to find two things you do EACH morning (shower and eat breakfast, for example) and take a few minutes with God between them. God wants to hear your voice and requests. He wants to remind you how much he loves you. He wants to spend a little time with you before you start your day.

MORE REFLECTION:

- "Very early in the morning, while it was still dark, Jesus got up, left the house and went off to a solitary place, where he prayed" (Mark 1:35).
- "I wait for the Lord, my soul waits, and in his word I put my hope. My soul waits for the Lord more than watchmen wait for the morning, more than watchmen wait for the morning" (Psalms 130:5-6).

FOR PONDERING FURTHER:

1. What keeps you from spending time with God in the morning?
2. What requests could you give God each day if He were to hear your voice in the first hour of awakening? (Think of short-term and long-term needs.)
3. Why do you think God wants to hear your voice rather than read your mind?

4. What is the psalmist "expecting" when he goes to God to make his requests?

LAST THOUGHT:
WOULD SPENDING A FEW MINUTES ALONE WITH GOD EACH DAY MAKE YOU MISS ANYTHING YOU WANT TO DO?

NINE

Aiming for the Target

Lord, who may dwell in your sanctuary?
Who may live on your holy hill?
He whose walk is blameless and who does what
is righteous, who speaks the truth from his heart
and has no slander on his tongue, who does his
neighbor no wrong and casts no slur on his fellow
man, who despises a vile man but honors those who
fear the Lord, who keeps his oath even when it hurts,
who lends his money without usury and does not
accept a bribe against the innocent. He who does
these things will never be shaken.
Psalms 15:1-5

Several passages of scripture seem to lay out a boatload of behavioral requirements for everyone to see. Taken at face value, these sections can seem discouraging. You may say to yourself: "If that's the kind of perfection it's going to take to get into heaven, I don't have a chance."

But God didn't put these passages in the Bible to exasperate you. He included them so you'd have something to aim for. It's true, passages like the one above sound all-inclusive. "Do these things and you'll be assured of getting in." But they weren't meant to be hard and fast rules to heaven. Instead, they show us God's moral target.

Does that mean you'll always hit it?

You know the answer to that one already—and so does God. There's no way on earth a human can ALWAYS hit the moral target. But there are several reasons to keep on trying, even if you've aimed in the opposite direction of the target a hundred times in a row:

It's the right target. By hitting the target, if only occasionally, you'll experience the rewards of being a good shot. There's an inner peace and a quiet confidence when you do the right thing. On the flip side, guilt, shame, and consequences you don't want to face are the "reward" when the target is deliberately and consistently missed.

It doesn't move. Moral targets have a tendency to shift and relocate based on whatever new fad, music group, or movie says is now the right target. That's why we have total moral confusion. Everyone seems to have an opinion on what's right and wrong. You can listen to them, of course, but get ready to face years of feeling as if you've never hit the bull's eye. God's target for sexual purity and other issues never change. That's good to know. You never have to wonder where to aim or which direction to go.

Others are motivated to aim for the same target. If you can do it, your friends can too. And if someone you know can hit the target, then YOU can. Success breeds success. In fact, trying to hit the target with others by your side, watching, cheering you on, giving you pointers is actually fun—and necessary. That's why being involved in a church or youth group is so essential. It gives you the assurance you're not the only one trying to hit a target that few are aiming at.

A close walk with Jesus Christ is your bull's-eye, but Scripture is filled with the outer rings of the target. If you keep Jesus in your sights, you'll never be too far away from the target.

MORE REFLECTION:

- "And do this, understanding the present time. The hour has come for you to wake up from your slumber, because our salvation is nearer now than when we first believed. The night is nearly over; the day is almost here. So let us put aside the deeds of darkness and put on the armor of light. Let us behave decently, as in the daytime, not in orgies and drunkenness, not in sexual immorality and debauchery, not in dissension and jealousy. Rather, clothe yourselves with the Lord Jesus Christ, and do not think about how to gratify the desires of the sinful nature" (Romans 13:11-14).

FOR PONDERING FURTHER:

1. Does God's target seem like an impossible one for you to hit? Why?
2. Why do you think so many Christian teens have such a tough time hitting God's target?
3. What are some of the ways you can practice hitting God's target?

LAST THOUGHT:

AIMING AT ANYTHING BUT GOD'S TARGET IS SIMPLY BAD MARKSMANSHIP.

TEN

Coming Full Circle

My God, my God, why have you forsaken me?
Why are you so far from saving me,
so far from the words of my groaning?...
For he has not despised or disdained
the suffering of the afflicted one;
he has not hidden his face from him
but has listened to his cry for help.
Psalms 22:1, 24

It's hard to believe that the two verses above are from the same psalm. In verse one, the writer is obviously wondering where in the world God is. By the time he gets to verse 24, he has come full circle. He knows God is listening.

This psalm is what is called a "messianic" passage. That means it directly refers to Jesus the Messiah. The words in the first verse are the same ones used by Jesus while he hung on the cross. He felt abandoned, so he said so. (The rest of this psalm has several references to the final hours of Christ that you will be familiar with.)

As a prophecy about Jesus, how do these verses and this psalm relate to you?

What if you were going through some tough times and needed to talk to your youth leader? When you called him, he told you he was in the middle of a huge project and wouldn't be able to meet with you until the next day. Would you conclude he *never* has time for you? Would you think he didn't care about you because he couldn't meet with you the exact moment you wanted? Or would you take it in stride, knowing your youth leader is a kind person and would talk with you immediately if he really could?

The answer depends on how well you know your youth leader.

Both the writer of this psalm and Jesus cried out to God. But neither cry seemed heeded by the One they wanted help from, at least not immediately. But they knew God's character, so they trusted Him. In this psalm, verse 24 is the conclusion of the writer. For Jesus, his conclusion came when he said, "Into your hands, I commend my spirit."

Both trusted the Father.

You wouldn't judge your youth leader by one brief no-show, but many people—including Christians—are quick to judge God by a situation they don't like. They don't wait to see the whole picture in order to come to the right conclusion about his true character. In essence, they cry out verse one, but never hang around long enough to get to verse 24. Those who do not follow God sometimes allow random occurrences to lead them to conclude that God doesn't exist or that he doesn't really care. They may ask questions like, "You say God is loving. You say God is in control. You say God has a reason for everything. Then why would He allow my six-year-old nephew to be run over by a car?" Or "If God is as good as you say he is, how could he sit by as six million Jews were killed in World War II?"

This world is filled with senseless acts of cruelty that truly make you think, *Where was God when all of this was going on?*

The Bible says that Satan is the prince of this world. But God certainly knows what's going on and can transform any bad situation into good. But because love demands the gift of freedom of choice, He chooses not to treat us as puppets. He allows evil-hearted people to do evil things. He even allows his followers to occasionally suffer—or to feel the suffering of others.

When this happens to you, you can get stuck on verse 1, wondering if there really *is* a God. Or you can trust his character enough to get to verse 24, realizing He truly is a loving God who is worth following and trusting.

MORE REFLECTION:

- "And we know that in all things God works for the good of those who love him, who have been called according to his purpose" (Romans 8:28).
- "For I am convinced that neither death nor life, neither angels nor demons, neither the present nor the future, nor any powers, neither height nor depth, nor anything else in all creation, will be able to separate us from the love of God that is in Christ Jesus our Lord" (Romans 8:38-39).

FOR PONDERING FURTHER:

1. Have you ever felt abandoned by God? When?
2. How would you describe your view of God's character during your growing up years?
3. Who do you know who you would say is a good representative of God's character?

4. What part of God's character (or His ways) do you find most troubling?

LAST THOUGHT:
TRUST IN THE TRUE CHARACTER OF GOD THAT YOU CAN SEE CLEARLY BY READING THE WHOLE BIBLE.

ELEVEN

Consider . . .

*When I consider your heavens, the work of
your fingers, the moon and the stars,
which you have set in place,
what is man that you are mindful of him,
the son of man that you care for him?
You made him a little lower than the heavenly beings
and crowned him with glory and honor.*
Psalms 8:3

Try this exercise: Close your eyes and think about the sun and stars, how big and awesome they are. Then consider the planets in the solar system. Now, picture the earth from outer space. See how huge and vast it is. Let your mind imagine each continent, each country, the big cities, the little towns, mountains, rivers, lakes, and farms.

Now, think about the variety of animals and fish God has made, how they exist and multiply and make the earth an incredible place to live.

Consider that though three-quarters of the planet is covered by water, and seven billion people occupy the land. How many is seven billion? How many more have lived and died through the centuries?

The number is awesome, yet God created them all. He understands the genetic code of each individual better than any scientist. After all, He thought it up. He knows the names of all people, their hopes and dreams . . . and their sins and evil desires. Yet he loves each soul more than you can ever imagine.

How much does He love, you ask? Picture Jesus Christ stretching his arms out as far as he can, looking into your eyes with love, then dying—FOR YOU.

That's how much.

MORE REFLECTION:

- "Consider the ravens: They do not sow or reap, they have no storeroom or barn; yet God feeds them. And how much more valuable you are than birds!" (Luke 12:24).
- "The earth is the Lord's, and everything in it, the world, and all who live in it; for he founded it upon the seas and established it upon the waters" (Psalms 24:1-2).

FOR PONDERING FURTHER:

1. What part of God's creation amazes you the most?
2. Why do you think teens rarely consider the intricacies of God's creation?
3. What would remind you to take a second and consider God's creation more often, appreciating him in the process?
4. Do you ever feel you're an insignificant part of the universe, or do you understand how special you are to God?

LAST THOUGHT:
BE FOREVER AMAZED BY WHAT GOD HAS CREATED.

TWELVE

The Joy of Possessing Nothing

*The wicked borrow and do not repay,
but the righteous give generously.*
Psalms 37:21

Have you ever given something you own—money, food, clothing—to someone else? Didn't it make you feel good?

If you're like most people, you rarely feel "righteous." Certainly, there are many believers who are self-righteous. That is, they view themselves as better than others. But most know the depths of darkness within their own hearts. To attach a word like *righteous* to themselves simply doesn't fit. The perceptive believer, however, knows that though he doesn't always *feel* righteous, he has been *made* righteous by what Jesus Christ has done.

This knowledge can be compared to not *feeling* like being a son or daughter to your parents, but *knowing* there is nothing you can do to change that fact. It's similar to not *feeling* like a Christian, but knowing you are one.

And what do the righteous do? They give . . . generously.

Money.

Time.

Possessions.

Talents.

Whatever you have, you know it's a gift from God. Since He is the original owner and is simply loaning it out to see what you'll do with it, He has every right to expect you to be a giver.

This doesn't mean you give *everything* away or that you give *every time* you're asked to. It means you're serious about being a generous Christian. It may mean not just giving away the stuff that's easy to part with. It sometimes means giving the best you own. Remember, God gave us his best. He gave . . .

HIS ONLY SON.

It was a thoughtful choice. A carefully weighed decision. He knew some would treasure this gift, and others wouldn't. But the reception or the gratefulness of the receiver wasn't God's motivation for offering the gift. The joy of giving was paramount in his mind.

Begin to practice living generously. Experience for yourself the joy of giving what you've been freely given: time, money (what little you may have), possessions, talents, forgiveness, and love.

MORE REFLECTION:

- "Remember this: Whoever sows sparingly will also reap sparingly, and whoever sows generously will also reap generously. Each man should give what he has decided in his heart to give, not reluctantly or under compulsion, for God loves a cheerful giver. And God is able to make all grace abound to you, so that in all things at all times, having all that you need, you will abound in every good work" (2 Corinthians 9:6-8).

- "A generous man will himself be blessed, for he shares his food with the poor" (Proverbs 22:9).

FOR PONDERING FURTHER:

1. What is easiest for you to give: time, money, possessions, or talents?
2. What makes the other things tougher to give?
   .Have you been generous with someone? What did you give and how did it feel?
3. Are you holding onto anything too tightly? If so, what would it take for you to recognize it as a gift on loan and not a possession to be hoarded?

LAST THOUGHT:

KNOW THAT YOU DO NOT OWN ANYTHING, AND THAT EVERYTHING YOU HAVE IS A GIFT.

THIRTEEN

These Opposites Don't Attract

You have not handed me over to the enemy
but have set my feet in a spacious place.
Psalms 31:8

The enemy in this passage isn't necessarily Satan, the spiritual adversary Jesus talked so much about. David was likely referring to an enemy who was trying to bury him in the hot sand in Israel. But just as David's enemy had a personality bent on evil and a strategy to destroy him, so your sworn enemy—Satan—has an evil strategy for you.

What should you do since you have so powerful an enemy?

Give up, throw in the towel, and go over to the other side?

Of course not!

Yes, Satan is powerful, smart, beautiful (so the Bible says) . . . and he hates you to the same degree God loves you. But all of his supernatural strength cannot compare to God's. Whatever strength the enemy has, the General on our side has more. The powers of darkness will never overcome the powers of light.

These two forces are exact opposites in strategy, goals, and tactics. Satan enslaves. God sets free.

Satan constantly tells you of your worthlessness. God—through his Word—constantly reminds you of your worth.

The Bible says God is love. What does that make Satan?

Do you get the picture? Satan has all that is evil at his disposal, but God has all that is good to help those who would call on his name.

There's one more exact opposite that is essential for the believer to know: Satan is called "the father of lies." God must therefore be the Father of Truth. Jesus was never intimidated by the power and influence of Satan (see Matthew 4) because he knew how to respond—with truth.

Satan rarely screams in a loud voice the lies he wants you to believe. He whispers:

"You'll never make it as a Christian at your school, so why try?"

"If you let someone else know you're a Christian, forget about ever having the right friends."

"Your parents are trying to make your life miserable with all of those rules. You need to push them more often to get them to bend."

When Satan whispers a lie, he knows that only one thing can destroy it: truth. And where is that truth found? David says, "a spacious place."

If you look out over your local football field from the top of the bleachers, you can immediately see how spacious it is. And when a game is going on, you can look from the same spot and see how each play develops—even better than the players on the field can.

God's truth found in His Word is that spacious place a Christian can go to find the right perspective, to perceive the big picture. In it you can see the whole truth of God's character, HIS game plan, and the truth about what He believes about you.

MORE REFLECTION:

- "The god of this age has blinded the minds of unbelievers, so that they cannot see the light of the gospel of the glory of Christ, who is the image of God" (2 Corinthians 4:4).
- "You, dear children, are from God and have overcome them, because the one who is in you is greater than the one who is in the world" (1 John 4:4).

FOR PONDERING FURTHER:

1. What lies has the enemy tried to tell you?
2. How did you respond?
3. What does God's Word say about you?
4. How does God protect Christians?

LAST THOUGHT:

KNOW THAT GOD'S TRUTH FOILS SATAN'S STRATEGY OF LIES.

FOURTEEN

The Classroom of Life

*For all can see that wise men die; the
foolish and the senseless alike perish
and leave their wealth to others.*
Psalms 49:10

David wasn't in graduate school when he wrote the above verse, but he hit on an essential point of living. "For all can see..." That is, "If you're alive, you should be able to grasp the fact that..."

He's saying that if you're alive, you'll learn. Perhaps not through books, but you'll notice things. To put it another way: If you live, you're a student. Period.

How good of a student do you want to be? This is the bigger question. How discerning are you about the important concerns of life? How motivated are you to use not only your brain to think things through, but your instincts?

The lesson David was referring to in this verse couldn't be learned simply through formal education. He had to be a "noticer" in order to truly GET IT. David *was* a noticer. He was perceptive, and he was a student of life and of people. He chose to take what he saw in the lives and hearts of those around him, compare that with what he knew and read about God, and (usually) come to the right conclusions. It wasn't a unique gift, but simply a matter of choice. And he wasn't mediocre at it either. He was GOOD.

The idea of being a lifetime student may not appeal to you, but accept it—you will be. Maybe not with books or formal education, but with people, life, and God's Word.

What kind of student do you want to be?

MORE REFLECTION:

- "The mocker seeks wisdom and finds none, but knowledge comes easily to the discerning. Stay away from a foolish man, for you will not find knowledge on his lips. The wisdom of the prudent is to give thought to their ways, but the folly of fools is deception" (Proverbs 14:6-8).
- "Instruct a wise man and he will be wiser still; teach a righteous man and he will add to his learning" (Proverbs 9:9).

FOR PONDERING FURTHER:

1. What or who has taught you the most about life?
2. How can you become a student of life?
3. Name some valuable things you've learned from the Bible.

LAST THOUGHT:

ALWAYS BE A LEARNER.

FIFTEEN

Taking It Personally

The law of the Lord is perfect, reviving the soul.
The statues of the Lord are trustworthy, making wise the simple.
The precepts of the Lord are right, giving joy to the heart.
The commands of the Lord are radiant, giving light to the eyes.
The fear of the Lord is pure, enduring forever.
The ordinances of the Lord are sure and altogether righteous.
They are more precious than gold, than much pure gold;
they are sweeter than honey, than honey from the comb.
By them is your servant warned;
in keeping them there is great reward.
Psalms 19:7-11

In reading this passage, the first question that may come to your mind is, "What Bible is this writer reading from?" He actually sounds as if he thinks God's Word is cool, doesn't he?

Then the thought could hit, *Oh, I get it! It was God who told the psalmist to write these words. No wonder it's in the Bible.*

Did the writer simply live in a different world than you? Was he a religious fanatic? Was his hand a pawn of the Holy Spirit, so he had no choice but to write those words?

If you said "yes" to all of the three previous questions, you've likely just given yourself permission NOT to understand the true depth of what God wants to tell you. From now on, you'll be able to see this passage (and probably others) and not grasp its significance to your life.

But let's assume you said "no" to one or more of them. That means you won't easily dismiss an important portion of Scripture. You figure it's OK to cut the writer some slack. You actually want to see what you can pull out of the passage. Sure, you know God inspired the psalmist to write it down, and he *did* live in a different century. But since nearly all of the other Bible writers were ordinary sinners, it's safe to assume he was too.

The question remains: How could the Bible have been so different for this writer?

First, *he likely had read it.* No, he didn't have the New Testament or any of the minor or major prophets to peruse. He may only have had the first five books, plus Proverbs, Job, Ruth, and a few others. But somewhere along the line, his first-person experience with it had been VERY positive. He hadn't just glanced through it once, but had likely read it—or heard it read—several times.

Second, *he had probably tested it.* When you hear facts about life, the first thing you might do is go out and see if they're actually true. *Do you really get cold if you only wear jeans and knit gloves instead of the proper clothing to the ski slopes? Will the car really quit running if the gas gauge gets below "E"? Would Dad dare take the car away if you came home an hour past curfew?* Sometimes all it takes is one test to find out that what you'd heard was true.

Third, *other people had tested parts he hadn't.* You don't have to test everything yourself. In fact, the wisest people are those who have learned from the mistakes of others, instead of making the same ones. They're those "noticer" types we talked about earlier.

The writer realizes that the Word of God is a love letter, not a rule book. He knows that only a cruel God would make people in his own image without leaving them an instruction manual. But with God's Word to guide us, we have a light to illuminate our path as we traverse all of the peaks and valleys of life.

Carefully read these verses a couple more times. What the writer has discovered you can know too. This fact isn't just for pastors, monks, or the learned. It's for the common follower of God.

MORE REFLECTION:

- "For the word of God is living and active. Sharper than any double-edged sword, it penetrates even to dividing soul and spirit, joints, and marrow; it judges the thoughts and attitudes of the heart" (Hebrews 4:12).
- "Now that you have purified yourselves by obeying the truth so that you have sincere love for your brothers, love one another deeply, from the heart. For you have been born again, not of perishable seed, but of imperishable, through the living and enduring Word of God. For, 'All men are like grass, and all their glory is like the flowers of the field; the grass withers and the flowers fall, but the word of the Lord stands forever.' And this is the word that was preached to you." (1 Peter 1:22-25).

FOR PONDERING FURTHER:

1. Does God's Word seem relevant to you personally?
2. What do most of your friends think of God's Word?
3. Why do you think some people are actually turned on by it?

LAST THOUGHT:
LOVING GOD AND GOD'S WORD IS A GAME-CHANGER.

SIXTEEN

He Knows Exactly

*I will be glad and rejoice in your love, for
you saw my affliction and knew the anguish
of my soul.*
Psalms 31:7

You can never accurately say to God, "You don't know what I'm going through!" If there is an emotion that you can experience, God knows it firsthand through His Son. Jesus experienced all the temptations and human feelings that you will ever know: anger, rejection, humiliation, exhilaration, depression, loneliness, perfect peace, love. If you've felt it, so has he.

And he knows—intimately—what anguish of the soul can do to a human. Jesus faced it in the garden of Gethsemane when he prayed, "Father, if you are willing, take this cup from me; yet not my will, but yours be done" (Luke 22:42). Jesus knew he would soon be bearing the sins of the entire human race on his body. But an even greater anguish came when he recognized that his Father had left him. While hanging on the cross, he cried, "My God, my God, why have you forsaken me?" (Matthew 27:46b).

For nine hours while Jesus hung between heaven and earth, his Father deserted him. The reason? Since God was sinless, He could not be in the presence of sin, and that's what Jesus became on the cross. "God made him who had no sin (Jesus) to be sin for us" (2 Corinthians 5:20a). He bore the weight of your sin in his body. Then he died, killing sin once and for all. Three days later he rose from the dead to show that sin and death were conquered, thus opening the door to anyone who would receive his finished work on the cross as payment for sin.

Anguish of the soul. Yes, Jesus knew it better than anyone who ever lived. The Father he had been with since the foundation of the world left him at his greatest hour of need. It was a joint plan hatched after Adam sinned, and the anguish was worse than we could imagine.

But what if Jesus hadn't tasted that total separation from God for those nine fateful hours nearly 2,000 years ago? Then WE would have . . . for eternity.

For Jesus, it was worth the anguish.

Knowing what he went through should give you the absolute certainty that your anguish—no matter how great—can never match his. Though your anguish is real—and sometimes unbearable, you'll think—he can relate. But even more, he can come to your rescue.

MORE REFLECTION:

- "For we do not have a high priest who is unable to sympathize with our weaknesses, but we have one who has been tempted in every way, just as we are—yet without sin. Let us then approach the throne of grace with confidence, so that we may receive mercy and find grace to help us in our time of need" (Hebrews 4:15-16).
- "Since the children have flesh and blood, he too shared in their humanity so that by his death he might destroy him

who holds the power of death—that is, the devil—and free those who all their lives were held in slavery by their fear of death.

"For this reason he had to be made like his brothers in every way, in order that he might become a merciful and faithful high priest in service to God, and that he might make atonement for the sins of the people. Because he himself suffered when he was tempted, he is able to help those who are being tempted" (Hebrews 2:14-15, 17-18).

FOR PONDERING FURTHER:

1. Have you ever felt as if no one could understand what you were going through?
2. Have you ever felt deeply anguished?
3. Is it easier or harder for you to approach God when something is troubling you?
4. Does knowing how much God loves you help when you're going through a trying time? How?

LAST THOUGHT:
KNOW THAT JESUS UNDERSTANDS WHAT YOU'RE GOING THROUGH, NO MATTER WHAT IT MAY BE.

SEVENTEEN

Where Heart and Tongue Meet

I will praise you, O Lord, with all my heart;
I will tell of all your wonders.
Psalms 9:1

In biblical days, talking about God and things He had done for you wasn't considered weird. In fact, if you *didn't* mention the Lord in conversation, *that* was thought to be odd. Back then, there was no shame or embarrassment in recognizing that an unseen God was active and at work among the nations.

Today, things have flip-flopped. Talking about a personal, loving, creative God brings strange looks, sometimes a little ridicule. Why is it often so difficult to talk about what is in our hearts?

Two reasons. First, our hearts aren't always filled with praise. The distractions and temptations, the pride and neglect, keep us as followers of God from realizing and acting on what we know. We know what God has done, but sometimes we don't think of it much or give Him the credit that is His due.

That leads to the second reason: If we don't think about it, why would we talk about it? It is only when we can praise God with all our heart that we would want to tell others about what God has done for us.

If we don't think of our sin—and what God did to remove it from us so we wouldn't have to pay the penalty for it—then we won't tell others of our Savior.

Telling others about the wonders of God starts by recognizing those wonders in your own life. Once the heart is in gear, then the tongue will likely follow.

MORE REFLECTION:

- "I will praise you, O Lord my God, with all my heart; I will glorify your name forever. For great is your love toward me; you have delivered me from the depths of the grave" (Psalms 86:12-13).
- "Then they called them in again and commanded them not to speak or teach at all in the name of Jesus. But Peter and John replied, 'Judge for yourselves whether it is right in God's sight to obey you rather than God. For we cannot help speaking about what we have seen and heard'" (Acts 4:18-20).

FOR PONDERING FURTHER:

1. Is it difficult for you to talk about God at school? At home?
2. Why do you think young people have difficulty telling others of their faith?
3. Have you ever told anyone of the "wonders" of God? What happened? How did you feel?
4. What "wonders" could you talk about?

LAST THOUGHT:
REMEMBER TO PRAISE GOD WHEREVER YOU ARE.

EIGHTEEN

"Could You Have a Bad Memory, Please?"

*Remember not the sins of my youth and
my rebellious ways; according to your love
remember me, for you are good, O Lord.*
Psalms 25:7

Most teens say things they don't mean, try things they know they shouldn't, and listen to voices that don't have their best interests at heart. Not every youth is reckless, nor are most ALWAYS rebellious. But as Proverbs 22:15 points out: "Foolishness is bound up in the heart of a child."

How do you deal with your own foolishness? Which of the following options would you choose?

A. If you're of a mind to be rebellious against your parents or the church, well, it's your mind. Perhaps your parents can control your outward behavior for a time through selective punishments. But they can't control your thoughts. In essence, you can be consistently sinful, and there isn't a lot anyone can do about it until you're ready to change.

B. You can use your behavior to your advantage whenever you mess up. You can say, "Even the Bible predicts I'm going to do stuff like this, so cool off, Dad." This may work—once. After that, however, your dad will start talking about deliberate choices and accepting responsibility, then you'll be stuck with punishments you won't like.

C. You could also make an effort not to sin. And when you fail (we all do), you can be humble, admit your mistakes, take responsibility for your actions, and ask for forgiveness. When you do this, something miraculous happens: sins are not only forgiven, they're also forgotten. Honest confession to those who love you have a way of cleaning the slate—completely.

Would David have made the statement in the above verse to God if he thought God wouldn't have honored it? Not likely. You see, he knew something remarkable about God's character. He likes to forget things. He is less interested in keeping track of your sins than your parents are. He would much rather start fresh and press on.

There is just one prerequisite: a humble heart filled with genuine repentance.

David was good at messing up, but he was even better at admitting it when he did (see Psalm 51). When he admitted his failures, God chose to have selective amnesia. This is another BIG reason why God is so good: He constantly chooses to clean the slate and *forget* our past mistakes.

MORE REFLECTION:

- "Flee the evil desires of youth, and pursue righteousness, faith, love, and peace, along with those who call on the Lord out of a pure heart" (2 Timothy 2:22).
- "Young men, in the same way be submissive to those who are older. All of you, clothe yourselves with humility toward

one another, because, 'God opposes the proud but gives grace to the humble.' Humble yourselves, therefore, under God's mighty hand, that he may lift you up in due time" (1 Peter 5:5-6).

FOR PONDERING FURTHER:

1. When you blow it in some way, what is your first reaction? Do you admit it to the right "authorities," or hide it?
2. What has happened to you at home when you admitted your mistakes? At school?
3. How do you feel when you try to hide your mistakes? How about when you confess?
4. Why do you think David would have the boldness to ask God to forget his sinful early years?

LAST THOUGHT:
REALIZE GOD BOTH FORGIVES AND FORGETS.

NINETEEN

Keep Your Reputation Strong

*For the sake of your name, O Lord, forgive
my iniquity, though it is great.*
Psalms 25:11

Unlike us, God isn't a people pleaser. He's done things—or been accused of doing things—that have made His creations angry at Him, shake their fists at Him, ignore Him for decades, and even actively work against Him and everything He stands for.

But God *is* zealous about one aspect of His reputation: being known as a forgiver.

You see, God has a reputation to uphold. And though he doesn't care about *everything* people think of him, he definitely wants his creation to understand this part of his character.

People are known by what they've done, good or bad. Usually the reputation is justified. Each of us earns the love, hate, or indifference others feel when they think about us. But how has God's reputation been established? By what he did in the Old Testament? For a few, perhaps. By what he did in the New Testament? Again, a few.

Today, God mainly gets his reputation from the way his kids (us) act.

If we act like snobs, those who have never met God think he's a snob.

If we act like rich white folk, people could think God is rich and white.

If we act confused about who we are as his children, God would be . . . confusing.

If we act too serious, God wouldn't be any fun.

If we act judgmental, God could be viewed as a harsh authority figure.

And if we act unforgiven, God would be seen as too perfect to relate to. Others wouldn't even try to get to know someone so unapproachable.

God longs for everyone to see His *true* character. He wants to be known as a God who forgives and forgets, who so longs for an open relationship with his creation that he would do anything to establish that relationship. He would even leave heaven, become one of us, live as a servant, and die like a criminal. All to prove once and for all that he can be trusted and loved.

When David prayed this prayer asking for forgiveness, he knew what was at stake. He didn't just want his sins wiped away. He also wanted God's true character to shine through to those around him. He wanted to *know* he was forgiven so he could *act* forgiven.

God wants you to know His forgiveness and love . . . and act like you know it. This is the only way He will be known for what He wants to be known for.

MORE REFLECTION:

- "When you were dead in your sins and in the uncircumcision of your sinful nature, God made you alive with Christ. He forgave us all our sins, having cancelled the written code, with its regulations, that was against us and that stood opposed to us; he took it away, nailing it to the cross" (Colossians 2:13-14).

- "Therefore, my brothers, I want you to know that through Jesus the forgiveness of sins is proclaimed to you. Through him everyone who believes is justified from everything you could not be justified from by the law of Moses. Take care that what the prophets have said does not happen to you: 'Look, you scoffers, wonder and perish, for I am going to do something in your days that you would never believe, even if someone told you'" (Acts 13:38-40).

FOR PONDERING FURTHER:

1. What is your reputation at school among those who know you?
2. How about for those who don't know you very well?
3. What have you done for God's reputation?
4. Is it important to you to have a good reputation?

LAST THOUGHT:

IF YOU KNOW YOU'RE FORGIVEN, YOU WILL MORE LIKELY BE ABLE TO ACT LIKE IT.

TWENTY

Embracing Both Inevitables

*Weeping may remain for a night, but
rejoicing comes in the morning.*
Psalms 30:5b

Two things you will know in life:

Valleys. Sometimes these will be the self-inflicted, "reaping what you sow" variety. Just as often it will be the "that's just the way life is" brand of pain. And, occasionally, it could be the "God-inflicted" discipline that seems painful, but is truly for your own good. Then comes the . . .

Mountaintops. You'll eventually get over the pain, out of the valley, and move on to greater heights.

Someone once said, "Life, even in America, isn't all Disneyland." Simple, true, but not a fact most of us like thinking about. We prefer to approach each day as if we're entering a new theme park. We resent it when unexpected misfortune ruins our fun.

While there will always be plenty of good times and mountaintop experiences, there are the inevitable valleys, as well. We can't escape the occasional night of tears, nor should we try. It is a trustworthy statement: "Grass doesn't grow on the mountaintop." You need the valleys to appreciate the exhilaration of the view from the pinnacle.

Breaking it down to where you may live: You may need to be without money once in a while so you'll be thankful you have an allowance at all. You may need to be grounded from the car keys so you'll know that driving is a privilege, not an inalienable right. You may need to get really sick to truly savor and be thankful for the gift of health.

All valleys—both in the topographical sense and in life—eventually lead back to the mountains. Yes, some hikes out of the valley are no longer than others, but the horizon will always, ALWAYS, be one day filled with terrain that will lead you out of the desolation that valleys seem to be. When you finally reach a height where you can see the valley below, see the place from which you came, you have the right to react a few different ways:

- *"I don't EVER want to be in that valley again."* It's OK not to want to experience the same discomfort twice.
- *"That was the toughest valley I've ever been in, but I sure learned a lot about hiking through life because of it."* It's essential that you learn the lessons of the valley the first time. You don't want to miss the maturity that comes, and thus have to endure a similar valley again.

As the psalmist says, the valley of tears last but for only a night. But rejoicing comes in the morning. The statement is accurate, but don't take it too literally. Remember, most pain isn't just for one night, and some hurts and pains could even last a lifetime. But there will be a morning when there are no more tears, a morning where the faithful will be able to see all things clearly.

Each new day brings that morning twenty-four hours closer.

MORE REFLECTION:

- "Jesus wept" (John 11:35).
- "Rejoice in the Lord always. I will say it again: Rejoice!" (Philippians 4:4).

FOR PONDERING FURTHER:

1. What are some things that have made you cry?
2. How long did the tears last?
3. What causes you to forget about past pains so you can enjoy today?
4. What would life be like if you only experienced the joys and no pain?

LAST THOUGHT:

BE CONFIDENT THAT ALL VALLEYS LEAD TO A MOUNTAINTOP.

TWENTY-ONE

"Hit Me With Your Best Shot"

*Test me, O Lord, and try me, examine
my heart and my mind.*
Psalms 26:2

Weightlifters know one important fact: you can't be built up until you're broken down. That's why they pump so much iron. The constant strain on their muscles breaks them down to the point where their muscles react by getting stronger. The "No Pain, No Gain," motto is apt. The strongest people in the world push their muscles to the limit.

In the same way, the strongest Christians in the world are those who have been pushed to the limit. Instead of praying for an easy life, one without trial and strain, they pray that when trials come, they will be strong in the Lord and in the strength of His might. That prayer is always answered.

And then there are . . . the "weightlifter Christians."

They don't simply go throughout the day hoping their muscles will be tested, they *intentionally* seek out chances to exercise, to push, to strain, to be torn down, if you will, so they can be built up to higher levels of spiritual strength.

Like David, they let God know they are ready to be tested ... tried ... examined.

They don't shy away from asking God to move them to the next level of maturity. They're not content to look like the rest, and they don't want spiritual muscles for the sake of vain competition. They want the extra power in order to be prepared for kingdom work. Once you've tasted being used by God to affect the spiritual destiny of another person, there is no greater mission to pursue or joy to be achieved. Nothing compares.

Asking God to test you is one of the most unselfish prayers a believer can pray. You're not asking God to help you skate through life until you enter the pearly gates. You're asking that your heart and mind be examined so that your motives are pure.

It's a challenge few take on.

It's a prayer few dare to pray.

Will you?

MORE REFLECTION:

- "Blessed is the man who perseveres under trial, because when he has stood the test, he will receive the crown of life that God has promised to those who love him" (James 1:2).
- "Not only so, but we also rejoice in our sufferings, because we know that suffering produces perseverance, perseverance, character, and character, hope" (Romans 5:3-4).

FOR PONDERING FURTHER:

1. What are the biggest tests that come into your life?

2. Do you wish they would all go away, or do you ever find yourself wondering if you have the strength to handle even more?
3. What would you call a "really tough trial"?
4. How can tests and trials make your faith stronger?

LAST THOUGHT:
GOD USES YOUR TRIALS TO STRENGTHEN YOUR SPIRITUAL MUSCLES.

TWENTY-TWO

What Type of Drowner Are You?

*In his pride the wicked does not seek him;
in all his thoughts there is no room for God.*
Psalms 10:4

Lifeguards on ocean beaches, those who save drowning people for a living, talk about three types of swimmers in trouble:

1. *The one who's drowning and knows it* (usually a female). This is the one who recognizes a need for help and lets a lifeguard do the job.
2. *The one who's drowning and knows it, but panics* and winds up almost drowning the rescuer (either male or female).
3. *The one who's drowning but doesn't recognize it* and tries to communicate to the lifeguard, "I can handle it" (almost always a male).

The "drowning difference" between males and females is an odd thing. Females usually recognize their need for help, while males tend to remain clueless—even as they're going under.

Pride is the killer.

The choice to stay in control can be the most dangerous one known to humankind. It's a burning desire that blinds us to the truth and encourages us to stick with the lie, no matter what the cost.

Some people choose to remain blinded their whole lives. Regretfully, these are the ones who pay the highest cost—spending eternity never knowing or recognizing how much God loves them, how much better it would be if HE were in control.

The psalmist says that the wicked don't even think about God. If not God, then what?

Themselves.

How to get their own immediate needs met.

How to stay in control.

How it will look if they admit they're in trouble.

Keeping their pride above all else.

God's love allows everyone—male and female—to have their pride, to hold it with a tight grip. Even until the end. Even in the face of eternal consequences. He loves all of his creation enough not to control them. It's the highest form of love there is.

MORE REFLECTION:

- "Pride goes before destruction, a haughty spirit before a fall" (Proverbs 16:18).
- "For everything in the world—the cravings of sinful man, the lust of his eyes and the boastings of what he has and does—comes not from the Father but from the world. The world and its desires pass away, but the man who does the will of God lives forever" (1 John 2:16-17).

FOR PONDERING FURTHER:

1. How do you think your pride affects your relationship with God?
2. What is "good pride"?
3. What do you believe to be "bad pride"?
4. Do you believe you have a problem with pride?

LAST THOUGHT:

DROP YOUR PRIDE—ESPECIALLY WHEN YOU'RE DROWNING.

TWENTY-THREE

Angels on Assignment

*For he will command his angels concerning
you to guard you in all your ways; they will
lift you up in their hands, so that you will not
strike your foot against a stone.*
Psalms 91:11-12

We don't know about their size, looks, or what they wear, but the Bible repeatedly talks about angels, so they must be real. Firsthand experience with an angel is nearly impossible to talk about unless you've seen one (which very few people have). This is a case where it's best to let the Bible talk about the facts.

They protect the believer.
"See that you do not look down on one of these little ones. For I tell you that their angels in heaven always see the face of my Father in heaven" (Matthew 18:10).

They can sometimes be seen.
"Do not forget to entertain strangers, for by so doing some people have entertained angels without knowing it" (Hebrews 13:2).

"But after he [Joseph] had considered this, an angel of the Lord appeared to him in a dream and said..." (Matthew 1:20).

They shouldn't be worshipped.

"Do not let anyone who delights in false humility and the worship of angels disqualify you for the prize. Such a person goes into great detail about what he has seen, and his unspiritual mind puffs him up with idle notions" (Colossians 2:18).

They can be counterfeited by Satan.

"For such men are false apostles, deceitful workmen, masquerading as apostles of Christ. And no wonder, for Satan himself masquerades as an angel of light" (2 Corinthians 11:14).

They aren't as important as Jesus.

"So he [Jesus] became as much superior to the angels as the name he has inherited is superior to theirs. For to which of the angels did God ever say, 'You are my Son; today I have become your Father'?" (Hebrews 1:4-5).

Like the wind, angels are always there, though you can't always see them. They are yet another way that God shows his love and care for his creation.

FOR PONDERING FURTHER:

1. What do you believe about angels?
2. Do your friends who don't follow Christ believe in angels?
3. Is there a way to recognize them more often (but not worship them) in your life today?
4. How can it help to know they are there?

LAST THOUGHT:
KNOW THAT IN THE UNSEEN REALM, ANGELS ARE BUSY ON YOUR BEHALF AND DOING GOD'S WORK.

TWENTY-FOUR

The Human Disease and Dis-ease

*The fool says in his heart, "There is no God."
They are corrupt, their deeds are vile; there is
no one who does good. The Lord looks down from
heaven on the sons of men to see if there are any
who understand, any who seek God. All have turned
aside, they have together become corrupt;
there is no one who does good, not even one.*
Psalms 14:1-3

It's not right to categorize people, but let's admit that we see the obvious types of people who walk the halls at every school:

There are those who look like they have it all together. They wear the right clothes, have a near-perfect complexion, have lots of friends, get good grades, and perhaps participate in sports or other activities. Let's call these the "popular" folks.

A few are the "shy" type. They don't fit in. They eat alone in the lunchroom, and it's tough for them to make eye contact with others.

The partyers at your school have a variety of looks. Some take care of themselves, some don't. That probably depends what kind of family they have.

There are several other in-between types, of course, that are tough to categorize. They have a look all their own.

A few questions: Who's better? Who is nicer to you? Who is less likely to cheat or put down someone else? Who wouldn't steal from a store if they got the chance?

The fact is, though everyone looks different from the outside, on the inside, everyone is pretty much the same. They all have the same potential to be jerks . . . as you do. David has pinpointed the reason why in this passage: "All have turned aside . . ." We're all sinners, and it's a disease we can't get away from. Because of what is inside us, all of us have the potential to do stupid stuff—no matter what we look like on the outside.

A few more questions: Does it ever bother you that it's tough to count on people—even friends—to treat you the way you want to be treated? Have you ever been treated better by those who *don't* go to church than by someone who *does?* When Christians treat you poorly, do you wonder how God will treat you? Do the consequences of a planet full of sinners sometimes make you wonder if God is really there? If you answered "yes" to any of these questions, then you know something of the human dis-ease.

What does God think about our disease and our dis-ease? He understands it completely, and He calls it like it is. Sin (the disease) and the consequences of our sin (the dis-ease), make it difficult for us to know God as He is. It's the reason He had to come down and live among us, to show us what He was really like. This is why He chose to die for us. He came to earth so we could see Him instead of just read about Him.

So we could know the truth about what He is truly like.

So we would understand that we really need Him—in this life and the next.

So our disease—and our dis-ease—could be cured for all eternity.

But God can't walk visibly by our side. We have to trust that He's there, believe what He's told us, and pursue Him as much as we can.

If you do this, you won't be a fool. Instead you'll get some relief from your dis-ease by experiencing a small part of what it must have felt like to see Him and touch Him. It's not what heaven will be like—you only get a glimpse, a small taste. That's all God can promise until you see Him face to face. Then your disease and your dis-ease will be totally cured.

MORE REFLECTION:

- "Now we see but a poor reflection as in a mirror; then we shall see face to face. Now I know in part; then I shall know fully, even as I am fully known" (1 Corinthians 13:12).
- "Then you will know the truth, and the truth will set you free" (John 8:32).

FOR PONDERING FURTHER:

1. Do you know anyone who says they don't believe in God? What are they like?
2. What are the things about being a Christian you doubt most?
3. Do you think God is angry or intimidated by your doubts?
4. What do you think this passage is really saying?

LAST THOUGHT:
TRY NOT TO LET YOUR DIS-EASE KEEP YOU FROM GOD.

TWENTY-FIVE

"If You're Going to Break Something..."

> *The sacrifices of God are a broken spirit; a*
> *broken and contrite heart, O God,*
> *you will not despise.*
> Psalms 51:17

In Old Testament days, people had to "pay" for their sins by sacrificing something. The blood of animals was used to cover their sins, if only temporarily. Not only were the Jewish people instructed to have something killed for their own sins, but each year at Passover the high priest would sacrifice an unblemished lamb for the sins of the entire nation. Again, the belief was that this washed away the sin and guilt, for a time.

Where did they get this idea? God gave it to them. He not only instructed the Israelites what to do for each individual sin, but for the sins of the nation as well (see Leviticus for much of the sacrificial laws).

What the Israelites didn't know was that God was simply setting them up for the ultimate sacrifice to remove sin for all time. It would be Christ's death and his shed blood that would take away the sins of not just the Jews, but the whole world, not just once a year, but forever. The message God was trying to communicate to His people—a message He is still communicating today—is that it's not OUR sacrifice He wants. This verse is another clue God gave that there was going to be a better way.

What is that way? And how does this relate to you today?

When you really blow it, what are you tempted to do? Well, if you're human, you want to make up for what you've done. And for some reason, you just don't feel right until you've "evened the score." That is, done something equally good for the bad you committed.

In this verse, God is saying, "Cut it out! When it comes to your relationship with me, you can *never* even the score. I already did that for you, so quit trying. What I really want from you is a broken and contrite heart."

God knows the heart is the center of your "feeler" (emotions) and your "chooser" (mind). He wants *you* to choose to turn from your own way . . . and love Him. Why? Because what He desires most is a relationship with you based on love, not guilt. He doesn't want you to always think you have to "do something" to earn what He has freely given.

With parents, teachers, coaches, and employers, you will often have to make sacrifices to prove your obedience, ability, commitment, and loyalty. Not so with God. The reason is that all of these attributes can be manufactured out of a sense of obligation to people. But God sees much deeper than outward obligation. He knows that having your heart is where the relationship really begins between you and Him. Being broken before Him—rightly recognizing the Creator-creation bond—helps you see it, too.

MORE REFLECTION:

- "Therefore, when Christ came into the world, he said: 'Sacrifice and offering you did not desire, but a body you prepared for me; with burnt offerings and sin offerings you were not pleased.' Then I said, 'Here I am—it is written about me in the scroll—I have come to do your will, O God.' ... And by that will, we have been made holy through the sacrifice of the body of Jesus Christ once for all" (Hebrews 10:5-7, 10).

- "Therefore, I urge you, brothers, in view of God's mercy, to offer your bodies as living sacrifices, holy and pleasing to God—this is your spiritual act of worship. Do not conform any longer to the pattern of this world, but be transformed by the renewing of your mind. Then you will be able to test and approve what God's will is—his good, pleasing, and perfect will" (Romans 12:1-2).

FOR PONDERING FURTHER:

1. Have you ever felt as if you had to "earn" the love of your parent?
2. If you had to earn your parent's love, how could it be done?
3. Do you ever try to "earn" God's forgiveness and acceptance?
4. What do you think a broken spirit and a contrite heart looks like?

LAST THOUGHT:

DON'T TRY TO OVERCOME YOUR FAILURES BY GOOD WORKS, BUT BY A BROKEN AND CONTRITE HEART.

TWENTY-SIX

He Always Answers

I call on you, O God, for you will answer me;
give ear to me and hear my prayer.
Psalms 17:6

Does God hear and answer ALL your prayers? The best way to answer this important question is to tell you what I said when I addressed this issue in one of my previous books called *Camp, Carwashes, Heaven & Hell*. Here is a brief paraphrase:

Yes, God hears and answers . . . in four ways:

1. *"Yes."* This is by far our favorite way to have our prayers answered. Yet if EVERY prayer were answered "yes," we'd be miserable. We'd get our good prayers answered, but also our selfish ones.

2. *"No."* Though not quite as popular as the first answer, "no" has some distinct advantages. "No" keeps us from getting things that are actually selfish requests. It protects us from an unhappy future and allows God to be God and us to be obedient followers. When He says "no," it's not simply to remind us who's boss. God says "no" out of genuine concern for the big picture of our lives.

It's tougher, but we ought to thank God as much for the nos we get from as the yeses.

3. *"Wait"* or *"Maybe."* Both sound much like the dreaded "Not until Christmas" response you may have heard from your parents. Remember when you wanted a new coat or toy or bike . . . in October? The standard response was that Christmas was "just around the corner." Sometimes you got what you wanted, sometimes you didn't.

4. *"I told you that already!"* A lot of times Christians pray for things that God has already said we shouldn't ask for. For example:

- *"God, make me popular."* (You're actually asking for approval of men, rather than God.)
- *"Lord, I want to be rich so I can give lots of money away."* (Remember, it's easier for a camel to go through the eye of a needle than for a rich man to enter the kingdom of heaven.)
- *"Father, change my appearance so I can like myself better."* (Read Psalm 139. You're pretty special already!)
- *"Jesus, should I tell Martha—whose parents are going through a divorce, who has talked about killing herself so they'd stay together, who has been experimenting with drugs—just how much you love her?"* (Do you really need to ask?)

Many of your prayers have already been answered. The answers are in black and white in that book by your bed. You don't need to pray about it . . . DO IT!

MORE REFLECTION:

- "If you remain in me and my words remain in you, ask whatever you wish, and it will be given you" (John 15:7).
- "Ask and it will be given to you; seek and you will find; knock and the door will be opened to you. For everyone who asks receives; he who seeks finds; and to him who knocks, the door will be opened" (Matthew 7:7-8).

FOR PONDERING FURTHER:
1. Can you think of a time when God said "yes" to something you requested? How about "no"?
2. Is there anything you're still waiting for an answer to?
3. What type of things do you pray for?
4. Do you ever get weary of prayer, wondering if God is really listening *or* answering?

LAST THOUGHT:
WORK TOWARD BEING COMFORTABLE WITH HOW GOD ANSWERS EACH AND EVERY PRAYER.

TWENTY-SEVEN

Waiting for Justice

But God will redeem my life from the grave; he will surely take me to himself. Do not be overawed when a man grows rich, when the splendor of his house increases, for he will take nothing with him when he dies, his splendor will not descend with him.
Psalms 46:16-17

No one ever said life was fair. In fact, it will often seem downright unfair. For example:
- Cheaters *do* get away with it . . . and often *do* prosper.
- Those with bad morals sometimes *do* get rich.
- Those who give generously are not always rewarded with more possessions to give away.
- The good sometimes *do* die young.
- Being honest *can* sometimes get you in trouble.
- Looks sometimes win out over brains.
- Guys who mistreat girls occasionally end up with the best-looking girlfriends.

- Parents who do almost everything right sometimes have kids who go astray.

The list is endless. And throughout your life you'll shake your head at the misfortunes of the weak and the fortunes of the strong. The rich get richer, while the poor get poorer.

Will it ever end?

Yes, it will.

Sometimes the justice will occur in this life. A corrupt leader will finally get what he deserves. But what is more likely—and more *certain*—is God's judgment on the other side of life. Jesus talked about it when he told the story of the rich man in hell and Lazarus, the starving, scab-infested poor guy now in heaven (see Luke 16:19-31). If you remember, Abraham answered the rich man from heaven by saying, "Son, remember that in your lifetime you received your good things, while Lazarus received bad things, but now he is comforted here and you are in agony."

Whether Jesus was saying the patriarch Abraham could actually talk to someone in hell isn't the point. The point is that God is the Great Equalizer. There is a judgment to face, and those who face it without Jesus Christ there to defend them, who can't say, "Your Son took the penalty for me," will face a very certain eternity—forever separated from the Father.

The payback will occur, most definitely. But our hearts shouldn't rejoice when another soul is lost forever. Though it may temporarily make us smile when we see the unrighteous get what they deserve, we need to remember that if God's grace had not been freely given, we would face the same judgment as those who don't know Christ.

MORE REFLECTION:

- "For we have brought nothing into the world, so we cannot take anything out of it either" (1 Timothy 6:7).
- "Be still before the Lord and wait patiently for him; do not fret when men succeed in their ways, when they carry out their wicked schemes. Refrain from anger and turn from wrath; do not fret—it leads only to evil. For evil men will be cut off, but those who hope in the Lord will inherit the land" (Psalms 37:7-9).

FOR PONDERING FURTHER:

1. In what ways do you think life is unfair?
2. How does it make you feel when you see evil prevail?
3. Do you pray for the unjust, hoping that their hearts will turn?
4. What part of this passage do you think is most important?

LAST THOUGHT:

BELIEVE THAT GOD'S JUSTICE WILL PREVAIL.

TWENTY-EIGHT

The Invited Ruler

*Keep your servant also from willful sins;
may they not rule over me. Then will I be
blameless, innocent of great transgression.*
Psalms 19:13

When a two-year-old walks out of a store with an unpaid-for candy bar because he wanted something sweet, he's probably unaware that he's just committed a crime. But when a sixteen-year-old does the same thing, it's petty theft. The cops are often called.

Fine lines. Christians walk them all the time. Every day you are faced with situations that call for a decision. Will you do the right thing? Or will you do what is acceptable in our culture and not worry about it? The decision will be yours. You'll either choose to sin or not to sin.

David, the writer of many of the psalms, knew intimately that sins are willful choices. The Old Testament tells us a lot about his exploits. Early in life, when he was a servant of Saul, he'd usually stay away from willful sin. But later, after he became king, David deliberately sinned against God. Why? One probable reason was he stopped praying the prayer in this verse. He stopped asking God to show him how to steer clear of deliberate sin.

Remember, it's your nature to sin. But it's a choice to follow through with it. Whether it's cheating at school, going too far physically with the opposite sex, lying, or using your mouth as a weapon to hurt others, you'll always face the challenge of willful sin.

One tragic thing about sin is that the more you make the choice to follow through with it, the easier it is to keep at it.

But what if you prayed this prayer several times a day: "Lord, keep me from willful sin, this day"? And what if you really meant it, too? You knew that willful sin wasn't any good for you, so you *really* wanted to keep it far from your life.

You wouldn't just be a goody-two-shoes. You'd have a clean walk with God. Not squeaky clean, but so clean you wouldn't have to keep asking for forgiveness for the same sins all the time.

Worth a try, don't you think?

MORE REFLECTION:

- "No temptation has seized you except what is common to man. And God is faithful; he will not let you be tempted beyond what you can bear. But when you are tempted, he will also provide a way out so that you can stand up under it" (1 Corinthians 10:13).
- "The Lord knows how to rescue godly men from trials and to hold the unrighteous for the Day of Judgment" (2 Peter 2:9).

FOR PONDERING FURTHER:

1. What do you think *willful* sin is?

2. Can you think of any examples of *unwillful* sin?
3. Do you know anyone whose sin rules them instead of them ruling their own lives?
4. How do you feel during times when you're doing well, not committing a bunch of willful sins?

LAST THOUGHT:
BEGIN ASKING GOD TO KEEP YOU FROM WILLFUL SIN.

TWENTY-NINE

Making the Grade

Why does the wicked man revile God?
Why does he say to himself, "He won't
call me to account?"
Psalms 10:13

Quick question: Does God have the ultimate supercomputer in heaven, able to track every good and bad deed, keeping score for all who have ever lived? Most people seem to think something along these lines. They believe that if they can do more good things than bad throughout their lives, then their heavenly train ticket will be stamped "Approved," and they'll walk on board. Some people think that if they just keep away from the REALLY BAD sins—murder, armed robbery, rape—then it doesn't matter what they do with the rest of their lives, that God will let them in because they're "not as bad as others."

But the "heavenly accountant" theory doesn't hold up to a test of Scripture. It's pass or fail all the way. Here's why:

- Either you have Jesus the Son, or you don't (see 1 John 5:11-13).

- There's no other name given among men by which we can be saved (see Acts 4:12).
- Jesus is the way, truth, and life. No man comes to Father but through him (see John 14:6).

For example, the thief next to Jesus on the cross didn't have another twenty years to tip the scales to make up for his deeds, but upon seeing this sinner's repentant heart, Jesus told him he'd be with him this day in paradise (see Luke 23:39-43).

If your bad actions in this life weigh in at 100 pounds and your good at ninety-nine pounds, the realization and acceptance of Jesus Christ as the one who has punched your ticket by his shed blood on the cross adds the 1,000-pound weight that makes heaven a sure bet.

Like the heat shield on the space shuttle as it goes through re-entry to the earth's atmosphere, the foundation of Jesus Christ is strong enough to withstand any temperature from this life to the next. But if Christ isn't there, or if there is any other weakness—our life, work, or soul could be burned away. For some Christians, like the thief on the cross, there will be no reward besides salvation.

The point is, your actions in this life DO matter. There will be an accounting for what you've done on earth. The reward on the other side—whatever that will be—is determined by how you build on that foundation while on earth.

MORE REFLECTION:

- "For no one can lay any foundation other than the one already laid, which is Jesus Christ. If any man builds on this foundation using gold, silver, costly stones, wood, hay or straw, his work will be shown for what it is, because the day will bring it to light. It will be revealed with fire, and the fire will test the quality of each man's work. If what he has built survives, he will receive his reward. If it is burned up, he will suffer loss; he himself will be saved, but only as one escaping through the flames" (1 Corinthians 3:11-15).

- "Surely the righteous still are rewarded, surely there is a God who judges the earth" (Psalms 58:11).

FOR PONDERING FURTHER:

1. How would you rather be graded in school, pass-fail or on a curve (comparing your grades with the rest of the class)? Why?
2. How do you think God grades?
3. How should He grade?
4. How could He grade to make it fair for everyone who has ever lived?

LAST THOUGHT:

GOD HAS ONE STANDARD TO GRADE US ON: JESUS CHRIST.

THIRTY

The Only Sure Thing

*Some trust in chariots and some in horses, but
we trust in the name of the Lord our God.*
Psalms 20:7

If you listed all the things and people you put your trust in, you could likely fill up a spiral notebook. It would range from the yellow lines on a four-lane highway that keep the dump truck on its side of the road to a tiny staple that holds forty hours of work on a term paper; from every kind of food in a can, box, or bag that you trust hasn't been poisoned to doctors and dentists who work on your body, sometimes inflicting pain to keep you from worse suffering.

Without thinking, you trust. Why is that?

Experience.

The objects of your trust have proven themselves trustworthy by fulfilling what it promised. Yes, the doctor's needle hurt, but it rid you of strep throat in less than a day. Yes, that yellow line doesn't look like it can keep back a ten-ton piece of machinery going 55 mph from smashing your mother's Honda into a pancake, but it always has. If eating out of a bag of potato chips made you sick a few times in a row, you'd avoid that brand forever. But it doesn't, so you don't.

Humans are a trusting bunch . . . to a point. We'll trust technology for nearly everything related to life on planet Earth. But when it comes to where we'll spend eternity, we'll believe most anything. We've been known to bow down to silver and gold, pray to man-made idols, sacrifice babies to demons, and worse. We've even been known to trust that good works, church attendance, or generosity can somehow entice God to like us enough that we'll end up in heaven.

You'll never trust in a chariot, and probably not a horse, but you'll be tempted to trust in only what you can see for most of your life. Whether it's money, education, the words of a strong leader, your mind, or your own feelings, all of these will fall short of assuring you that God loves you and is watching over you . . . and has secured an eternal home for you with him. Only one thing can do that: Jesus Christ's death on a cross and resurrection from the dead.

You didn't see it. You can't duplicate it. But it is—to be sure—the ONLY way to heaven.

MORE REFLECTION:

- "You shall have no foreign god among you; you shall not bow down to an alien god" (Psalm 81:9).
- "And this is the testimony: God has given us eternal life, and this life is in his Son. He who has the Son has life; he who does not have the Son of God does not have life" (1 John 5:11-12).

FOR PONDERING FURTHER:

1. Name five things or people you trust implicitly.
2. Why is that trust so firm?
3. When it comes to securing an eternal destination, what do people tend to trust most?

4. What or whom do you trust most?

LAST THOUGHT:
PUT YOUR TRUST IN GOD ALONE.

THIRTY-ONE

He'll Never Leave

But Though my father and mother forsake me,
the Lord will receive me.
Psalms 27:10

Few of us know what it's like to be completely abandoned. Though many families have had one parent leave, rarely do both die at once or abandon their kids altogether. Most have at least one parent they can count on. But what emotions would be churning inside if you were to suddenly wake up and find not one, but both parents gone? Your first thoughts would be, *Who's going to take care of me?*

There's another type of abandonment that's more likely to occur—*emotional* abandonment. Parents who abuse alcohol or drugs, or who can't cope with pain in their own lives, or who choose to work long hours instead of investing their time in their children, can make a child feel just as abandoned as if a parent had physically left the home.

The worse of the worst—total emotional abandonment—is what the psalmist is referring to. "Though my mother and father forsake me . . ." Intentional and willful abandonment. When both parents die, there's nothing a child can do. And when one parent leaves, most of the time the motivation isn't to inflict pain on the child. But being deliberately forsaken could cause more hurt than most could bear.

Rest assured, God would never control circumstances by making your parents leave you. What you need to know most of all, however, is that, even if you feel abandoned by your parents, God will NEVER leave. God will always faithfully stick by his promises and stay close to anyone who calls out to him.

MORE REFLECTION:
- "Surely I [Jesus] am with you always, to the very end of the age" (Matthew 28:20b).
- "Be strong and courageous. Do not be afraid or terrified because of them, for the Lord your God goes with you; he will never leave you nor forsake you" (Deuteronomy 31:6).

FOR PONDERING FURTHER:
1. Do you remember a time when you were little when you got lost or felt abandoned? What happened?
2. Have you ever thought about what you would do if your mom and dad weren't around?
3. How confident are you about God's presence with you at all times?
4. What type of comfort does that bring?

LAST THOUGHT:
KNOW THAT GOD WILL NEVER LEAVE YOUR SIDE.

THIRTY-TWO

Free Road Maps, Anyone?

*Show me your ways, O Lord, teach me your
paths; guide me in your truth and teach me,
for you are God my Savior, and my hope is
in you all day long.*
Psalms 25:4-5

Has your family ever gone on a vacation without a road map or GPS? Have you—or your dad—ever driven around a city you're not familiar with, trying to find a location you've never been to? Have you ever been lost?

If you have a smartphone with GPS or Google Maps, you can pinpoint exactly where you want to go, choose the best route, and usually arrive on time.

There are many destinations human pursue: money, pleasure, fame, love, security, "enlightenment." And the road map for those destinations isn't a loving God or His holy Word. It's things as shallow as a TV personality, a movie storyline, a musician's lyrics, a magazine's allure, or an athlete's performance. Some of these destinations have a measure of worthiness; many don't. They falsely promise security, a future, and peace of mind.

What the human soul longs for is to arrive at a destination that will truly refresh and satisfy. And not at some point way off in the future . . . today. It's not the sense of having finally "arrived," but the confidence that you can be content and happy where you are this very moment—no matter where you are on the map.

Many destinations promise this type of inner confidence, but only one delivers.

Knowing God's ways, following closely to His path, walking daily with Him in full assurance that He is staying with you stride for stride . . . this is the only daily destination that satisfies the soul and fills a life with hope.

"Show me your ways, teach me your paths . . ." is a prayer God delights in answering. And the way He leads a follower on his path varies. He'll use His Word, His people, an "inner nudge." He's creative! Go ahead, test Him and see how He does. Give Him ninety days of undivided devotion and see where He leads.

MORE REFLECTION:

- "You have made known to me the path of life; you will fill me with joy in your presence, with eternal pleasures at your right hand" (Psalms 16:11).
- "The Lord will guide you always; he will satisfy your needs in a sun-scorched land and will strengthen your frame. You will be like a well-watered garden, like a spring whose waters never fail" (Isaiah 58:11).

FOR PONDERING FURTHER:

1. How often do you pray or think a prayer like the one in Psalms 25:4-5?
2. How do you think your life would change if you allowed God to guide you?
3. Can you think of a time when you felt God was leading you?
4. What does it "look like" to hope in God all day long?

LAST THOUGHT:

STICK CLOSELY TO GOD'S PATH.

THIRTY-THREE

Casting Worries Aside

*Cast your cares on the Lord and he will
sustain you; he will never let the righteous fall.*
Psalms 55:22

Have you ever had someone take a problem off your hands? "Oh, I'll handle it, don't worry," a friend says as he walks into the principal's office to explain what really happened out in the parking lot after the game, how he was an eyewitness to what happened: He saw that it wasn't your fault you backed over the fire hydrant. It was snowing, and "friends" were saying you were in the clear—as a joke—and had actually let you drive into the hydrant on purpose.

Or you're worried your dad is going to hit the roof because you pulled a C in advanced algebra when your progress report was at a B-plus. And since he wants you on the honor roll every time—and to attend the same private college *he* went to—you know that every one of your privileges is going to be taken away. But then Mon listens to you explain why you got the C (before Dad gets home), understands, then says, "Don't worry about your father, I'll keep him calm."

Worry. Anxiety. Problems. Big stuff or little stuff, it seems life comes gift-wrapped with tons of things that are beyond your control. And *that's* the problem: A lot of life *is* beyond your control! So the natural response is to lie awake nights and think about them.

Does a Christian have to be bound by constant worry? Besides heaven, isn't there ANY advantage to being a follower of Christ in *this* life?

That depends on how trusting you are.

Certain problems you cause on your own. And once you recognize the mess you're in, there usually will be a few choices for your next action. Most often, one choice will be the *right* step, and the others will be the *easier* steps. Examples: missing curfew, blowing an assignment, forgetting to do your chores, a friend getting angry at you because she heard about a few things you said about her while she wasn't around. *The solution:* Always trust the truth and take the *right* step.

Other problems will be WAY beyond your control. They'll come out of nowhere. You didn't cause them, and most of the time there's nothing you can do about them besides worry . . . or pray. Examples: parents' divorce, family financial reversal, an ill sibling, or your own illness. The solution: worry to the point of giving yourself an ulcer, so the attention will be on *you.*

Not exactly.

Prayer is the key. But not the wimpy kind of prayer where what you're asking for you've already convinced yourself won't happen. What's needed is the assurance that what you are holding onto (worry) can be taken out of your hands and firmly placed into the BIG hands of a caring Father. Pray this: "God, this problem is too big for me to handle. Here . . . You take it." It's effective to close your eyes and imagine yourself actually letting go of it with all ten fingers, then turning and walking away. Finally, you must constantly fight the urge to go back to God and say, "You're not powerful enough to deal with this problem, so I'll take it back." Sometimes this battle is daily, hourly, or minute by minute.

When problems you didn't cause come into your life, you've got to look them in the eye, realize who's on your team, and say, "Let the battle begin."

MORE REFLECTION:

- "Cast all your anxiety on him because he cares for you" (1 Peter 5:7).
- "Let us then approach the throne of grace with confidence, so that we may receive mercy and find grace to help us in our time of need" (Hebrews 4:16).

FOR PONDERING FURTHER:

1. What do you worry about most?
2. When you are anxious about something, how do you respond?
3. When others you know worry, does it help?
4. What do you think the Bible means when it says, "he will never let the righteous fall"?

LAST THOUGHT:

CONSIDER ALLOWING GOD TO HANDLE ALL THE PROBLEMS THAT ARE BEYOND YOUR CONTROL.

THIRTY-FOUR

What's Your Rep?

*May those who hope in you not be disgraced
because of me, O Lord, the Lord Almighty;
may those who seek you not be put to shame
because of me, O God of Israel.*
Psalms 69:6

Ever heard of the phrase "guilt by association"? It means you're judged negatively by those you spend your time with.

If you're not a smoker or a partier but hang out with those who are, people who don't know you will naturally assume you are a smoker or partier, just like your friends. And even if you tell them you don't smoke or drink and are just spending time with these people because you like them, most people won't believe you.

Jesus had the same problem. He spent time with prostitutes and tax collectors (those who were considered the scum of the earth), so the religious leaders concluded he must be just as evil as they were. As we know, their conclusions were dead wrong.

Though we hate being typecast because of the people we spend some time with, it's next to impossible to escape the roles people naturally put us in.

King David knew how important his reputation was. He knew God would be judged by David's association with *Him*. Everyone was well aware that David was a follower of God . . . and far from perfect. And since the king was such a public person, he also knew that outsiders—and even insiders—would judge the character of God by how David behaved as ruler. The pressure was on, and he pleaded with God not to let him blow it.

God realizes we're going to fail, but that will never keep Him from wanting to hang out with *us*. When you choose to call imperfect people your children, you leave yourself open to ridicule. God has proven through the centuries that if we're trying to be loyal to Him, He'll forever be loyal to us.

How should we respond to such loyalty? The only way we can: appreciatively, prayerfully, and with behavior that truly doesn't give Him a bad name (but realizing it sometimes will).

MORE REFLECTION:

- "You yourselves are our letter, written on our hearts, known and read by everybody. You show that you are a letter from Christ, the result of our ministry, written not with ink but with the Spirit of the living God, not on tablets of stone but on tablets of human hearts" (2 Corinthians 3:2-3).
- "Brothers, choose seven men from among you who are known to be full of the Spirit and wisdom . . ." (Acts 6:3a).

FOR PONDERING FURTHER:

1. What kind of reputation do you want to have at school?
2. To those who don't know you very well, what do you think is *your* reputation?
3. How would people at school characterize you as a Christian?

4. How is God's reputation affected by your behavior?

LAST THOUGHT:
KNOW THAT GOD WILL BE LOYAL TO YOU, EVEN IF YOU'RE SOMETIMES NOT LOYAL TO HIM.

THIRTY-FIVE

What Are You Afraid Of?

*I sought the Lord, and he answered me;
he delivered me from all my fears.*
Psalms 34:4

Fear is one of those emotions that is both natural and learned. It's natural to be afraid of falling off a 500-foot cliff to jagged rocks below. Even a child can predict the mess it would make. But being afraid of a "talking" skeleton is a learned fear. When you were young, someone or something *taught* you skeletons were scary.

Fear, both real and imagined, can cause people to do strange things. People can have phobias about almost anything. Fear of germs can cause someone to constantly wash his hands. Fear of the sun keeps a person from going outside.

Most of us, however, aren't controlled by irrational fears. There are too many other VERY REAL fears that have potential to control a Christian teen every day:

Fear of the crowd: More directly, fear of being the object of ridicule by those you view as important to your social survival. Teens are rarely comfortable enough with who they are that they don't care what others think. Some are so controlled by this fear that they'll betray what they know is true in order to be accepted. This type of fear is a fast-moving whirlpool that often leads down the drain. Once you get caught in this current of pleasing others to fit in, it's tough to swim to safer waters.

Fear of silence: How often do you actually sit in silence and think? Is it nearly impossible for you to do anything at home without your iPod hooked to your ears, a TV on, or some other electronic device filling the air with sound? Sitting in silence isn't easy because you have to be alone with your thoughts, your inconsistencies . . . yourself. This particular fear isn't outwardly frightening, but everyone knows it's inwardly true. Naturally, you're likely to keep yourself away from things you fear. So you push aside any thoughts about changing your behavior or charting a future direction in your life.

Fear of true communication: Guys especially have a hard time opening up. Somehow, they think, it's a sign of weakness to admit an area of need or a failure. So they clam up. A few years of keeping people at arm's length is all it takes to develop this type of behavior. What starts as a perceived fear becomes a lifestyle.

There are other fears, of course. So what's the answer? Seeking God, and asking Him to replace your fears with faith. Fear controls, but faith sets free. Which would *you* rather be, controlled or free?

MORE REFLECTION:

- "The Lord is my light and my salvation—whom shall I fear? The Lord is the stronghold of my life—of whom shall I be afraid?" (Psalms 27:1).
- "Do not be afraid of those who kill the body but cannot kill the soul. Rather, be afraid of the one who can destroy both

soul and body in hell. Are not two sparrows sold for a penny? Yet not one of them will fall to the ground apart from the will of your Father. And even the very hairs of your head are all numbered. So don't be afraid; you are worth more than many sparrows" (Matthew 10:28-31).

FOR PONDERING FURTHER:
1. What are you afraid of that you *should* be afraid of?
2. What do you fear that you probably *shouldn't* fear?
3. How have you rid yourself of childhood fears?
4. What do you think parents fear?

LAST THOUGHT:
ALLOW GOD TO TURN YOUR FEARS TO FAITH.

THIRTY-SIX

The Patient Heart Changer

From heaven the Lord looks down and sees all mankind; from his dwelling place he watches all who live on earth—he who forms the hearts of all, who considers everything they do.
Psalms 33:13-15

*O*mniscience. It means God knows everything. Of all of the words and concepts in the Bible, this may be one of the most difficult to grasp. If God knows everything, then He must know about the plans in the hearts of mass murderers. He must see the evil behind the movie and pornography industry. He must know who the child molesters and rapists are. And He also knows which hearts are going to be captivated by the powers of darkness to the point of wanting to become a practicing Satanist.

He knows the ugliness in the hearts of people. So why doesn't He DO something about all of this blackness and evil? Can't He just think them out of existence so they won't harm anyone ever again? And if

He won't obliterate them, why doesn't He just clean out the mess in those dirty hearts and make them be more loving?

Because . . . that's not God's way.

Annihilation or a complete and instantaneous heart overhaul is most likely the way YOU would deal with the bad apples, right? It's a good thing you're not God. You'd be zapping people the moment they stepped out of line, never giving them a chance to change. But God sees the long view. He "considers" everything we do. That's why He chooses to go about changing the world through loving the evil out of dark hearts.

Here's a good illustration of why God doesn't force His love on the hearts of men:

Most parents KNOW when their child's heart is far from them. But can they spank that child into loving them more? Can they lecture the child into obeying? Can they withhold every privilege until they get that hug they long for? They can, but they know it won't capture their child's heart. Only love can do that.

And since God knows everything, He knows this fact about the human heart. That's why He chose the strategy He did. He looked down from heaven, saw what was within our hearts, knew He had but a single option, and made the only choice His character would allow: He had to show his creation the depth of that love so they would be drawn to the light more than the darkness within. He had to die for them.

So how does God get through to the evil hearts who need to know his love?

Through the hearts and lives of those who have been touched by that love: yours and others who know Him.

MORE REFLECTION:

- "But the Lord said to Samuel, 'Do not consider his appearance or his height, for I have rejected him. The Lord does not look at the things man looks at. Man looks at the outward appearance, but the Lord looks at the heart'" (1 Samuel 16:7).
- "Therefore, if anyone is in Christ, he is a new creation; the old has gone, the new has come!... We are therefore Christ's ambassadors, as though God were making his appeal through us. We implore you on Christ's behalf: Be reconciled to God" (2 Corinthians 5:17, 20).

FOR PONDERING FURTHER:

1. How do you feel about the fact that God is watching everything you do?
2. Do you really believe God is aware of the evil in the world?
3. Are parents like this sometimes?
4. Why do you think some people are evil-hearted and some good-hearted?

LAST THOUGHT:
TRUST THAT GOD KNOWS HOW TO CHANGE HEARTS.

THIRTY-SEVEN

Bridge Builder

*Consider the blameless, observe the upright;
there is a future for the man of peace.*
Psalms 37:37

Have you heard the phrase, "Build bridges, don't burn them"? Burning a relational bridge means allowing the positive points of contact between you and someone else to deteriorate, as though they were reduced to cinders. Selfish humans don't care about keeping bridges intact, only about speaking their minds, saying what they feel, and not worrying about the mess it makes. They don't consider forgiving or seeking forgiveness. And if they allow relational bridges to go down in flames with another human whom they can see, they will most certainly do it with God whom they cannot see. That's why there is no future for the man who cares little about building bridges or about peace.

What does it mean to be a man or woman of peace? Why would Jesus call you "blessed" and a "son of God" if you are a peacemaker (see Matthew 5:9)? Because peace is at the very core of God's character. Remember, God went to great lengths to make peace between Himself and you. He chose to allow His Son to die to atone for your sinful nature. That word *atone* literally means to place "at one." When two entities are one, they are at peace, and there is no division.

As a follower of Christ, you aren't asked to be a people pleaser; you're challenged to be a peacemaker. And it is genuinely a HUGE challenge. Why? Honestly said, there are a lot of people in the world who are easier to ignore than to love. It feels good to burn the bridge rather than make the effort to make peace or build a bridge.

Believers don't have the luxury of burning bridges. The reason, of course, is that the cost of allowing your pride to burn a bridge is too high—someone else may miss heaven!

God has strategically placed you in the world to model His character before those who have not yet trusted in Jesus Christ. There are those in your sphere of influence who are easy to love and many who aren't. But God makes no distinction about whom you should be at peace with. In fact, He says if you can't love another human standing right in front of you, you can't really love Him whom you have never seen (1 John 4:20).

It's the effort at making peace, not the results God is so concerned with. Some people, no matter what you do in trying to repair a bridge, will turn and throw something combustible on it.

When you drop your pride and do all that you can to make peace—to douse the flames—you're doing what God has done with you. Remember, God knew that not everyone would accept the peace offering of His Son, but He knew He had to make an "above and beyond" effort.

Good thing He did.

MORE REFLECTION:

- "If it is possible, as far as it depends on you, live at peace with everyone" (Romans 12:18).

- "Whoever of you loves life and desires to see many good days, keep your tongue from evil and your lips from speaking lies. Turn from evil and do good; seek peace and pursue it" (Psalms 34:12-14).

FOR PONDERING FURTHER:

1. How easy is it for you to make peace with others?
2. How do you feel when someone tries to make peace with you?
3. Are you at peace with God?
4. Is there anything you need to do to be at peace with someone else? When will you attempt to make that peace?

LAST THOUGHT:
DO ALL YOU CAN TO KEEP PEACE WITH OTHERS.

THIRTY-EIGHT

The Evil Called Good

*The wicked freely strut about when what
is vile is honored among men.*
Psalms 12:8

When Tiffany spoke up in class about how she feels abortion is wrong because God creates all life, half the class—and the teacher—laughed at her.

When Ray told his friends on the team to stop talking about the different girls who'll have sex with them, his buddies called him a "fag."

Our world has always tolerated evil by trying to twist the truth about what—and who—it represents. For centuries, men have tried to call "evil good and good evil." The reason? If they can blur the lines between good and evil so that evil doesn't look so bad, then they can continue sinning without feeling bad about it. They can strut their wickedness in front of everyone without fear of being asked to change.

Those who have faith in Christ, however, know the source of evil—and it IS bad. But there is a temptation to keep quiet about it, to NOT call the bad that people do what it actually is—evil! And if you can't tell the truth about evil, it makes it much easier to fall into it yourself.

What does the Bible say about evil? It's essential to know that the Bible says MUCH about it. Here is a sampling:

We're to turn from it: *"Turn from evil and do good; seek peace and pursue it"* (Psalms 34:14).

We're to hate it: *"Let those who love the Lord hate evil, for he guards the lives of his faithful ones and delivers them from the hand of the wicked"* (Psalms 97:10).

"Let not my heart be drawn to what is evil, to take part in wicked deeds with men who are evildoers; let me not eat of their delicacies" (Psalms 141:4).

We're to recognize the days are evil: *"Be very careful, then how you live—not as unwise but as wise, making the most of every opportunity, because the days are evil"* (Ephesians 5:15-16).

We're to pray for deliverance from it: *"And lead us not into temptation, but deliver us from the evil one"* (Matthew 6:13).

We're to overcome it with good: *"Do not be overcome by evil, but overcome evil with good"* (Romans 12:21).

We're to stay away from it: *"Avoid every kind of evil"* (1 Thessalonians 5:22).

We're to know that if we have Christ, we have overcome the evil one: *"I write to you, young men, because you are strong, and the word of God lives in you, and you have overcome the evil one"* (1 John 2:19).

Evil acts, done by evil people, controlled by the evil one . . . will be everywhere you go. Since God chose to leave you in the world instead of taking you to heaven the moment you first trusted Him, He must know something you don't. The mission to love others—especially those who are bound by evil—is a high calling. It's the work God has left you here to do. But not with an attitude that sets you above everyone else. Instead, you're challenged to confront and overcome evil the way Jesus and the early Christians did: by acts of love, words of truth, and using the power of the Spirit.

FOR PONDERING FURTHER:

1. What evil have you seen in your life?
2. What do you think about it?
3. Have you ever confronted or challenged it in any way?
4. What would happen if you did?

LAST THOUGHT:
STRIVE TO KNOW THE DIFFERENCE BETWEEN GOOD AND EVIL.

THIRTY-NINE

Once You've Truly Known Him...

> *Better is one day in your courts than a thousand elsewhere; I would rather be a doorkeeper in the house of my God than dwell in the tents of the wicked.*
> Psalms 84:10

If you've never truly KNOWN God, this probably seems like an odd verse. Is David referring to sitting a whole day in church, versus spending a lifetime in Las Vegas . . . or Hawaii . . . or the French Riviera?

Think. What is in God's courts or the house of God?

God.

His presence.

"What's such a big deal about that?" you may wonder.

David is saying, "If you KNEW God, you wouldn't ask."

Imagine knowing that the Creator God, the Holy One, the Majestic Redeemer was actually right next to you, yes, inside of you. Even if you only experienced that wonder for but one day of your life—what would that do to your mind?

Once you've truly KNOWN that wonder, you understand. And nothing else comes close.

Have you noticed there has been a word conspicuously absent from this devotion so far? That word is *feeling* or *felt*.

Though some can occasionally "feel" that God is with them, He isn't a feeling. When you're walking down a mountain with a friend after spending a day at the top, do you "feel" that person or just know he's there? (True, if you're holding hands with your friend, it could be said that you feel him. But let's assume there is no physical contact.) You've just spent a great day with your friend, enjoying creation. You've had several meaningful conversations. It's been a blast. A year later, what will you say to your friend as you look back on that day? To be sure, you may say it was a good feeling to be with him. But more likely, you'll say, "Remember that time we hiked to the top of Skinner's Butte? That was a great day."

Your day with your friend may have felt good, but it wasn't a feeling; it was a fact, an inescapable memory of being together, knowledge that someone was with you that you cared about and who cared about you.

Having one day like that with God, David says, is worth trading every valuable baseball card you own, worth giving up Friday night dates for the next five years, and worth much more than any high that any activity could conjure up.

It's not a feeling, not an experience. It's simply being with God. It's everything from giving Him a small portion of your morning to visiting with Him for an entire day as you walk the sandy beaches on a deserted shoreline. It's reading a Christian book, or, yes, listening to a sermon in church from a fellow traveler who has walked a bit longer with God than you.

MORE REFLECTION:

- "I know that my redeemer lives, and that in the end he will stand upon the earth" (Job 19:25).
- "I am the good shepherd; I know my sheep and my sheep know me—just as the Father knows me and I know the Father—and I lay down my life for the sheep" (John 10:14).

FOR PONDERING FURTHER:

1. Have you ever "felt" God's presence?
2. Is that important to you?
3. What if you never "felt" Him again? Would that change your relationship with God in any way?
4. Why do you think David would say that one day with God is better than a thousand days without Him?

LAST THOUGHT:

DON'T RELY ON YOUR FEELINGS, BUT ON KNOWING GOD.

FORTY

A Miraculous Mystery

*From birth I was cast upon you; from my
mother's womb you have been my God.*
Psalms 22:10

Life is precious to God. Anything He creates is important to Him, but human life is most valuable of all. We are the only creatures who were made in His image. Miraculously, He has chosen to give human beings a spirit, something invisible that lives forever. It's temporarily housed in a fragile earthsuit that is susceptible to car crashes, cancer, drug overdoses, and manmade mechanisms of war. But amidst all of the ways man has found to kill the earthsuit, it is still fairly resilient.

To Jesus, the body was important. Otherwise he wouldn't have spent so much time healing those whose earthsuits had malfunctioned. But there was more. He knew that sin had the power to make what was originally intended to be alive . . . dead. Namely, our spirits.

As the invisible breath of God meets the egg and sperm in secret, a life is formed. It is something God becomes instantly personal with. "From my mother's womb you have been my God," David says.

A spirit created, temporarily clothed in an earthsuit, incubating until ready to breathe real air, eat real food, and love his or her Creator.

Miraculous.

The starting point isn't at birth, nor is it at some predetermined age of accountability, but in the womb.

Why was this important for David to know? Why is it essential for you to know?

At some point, you'll think, *Why am I here?* Or even, *Why do things happen the way they do?* David's declaration points to the answer. It's so you'll know who your Father is and trust that He knows the smallest details of your life—and the lives of all who have lived. The "why" questions pale in importance when you've settled the "who" question.

There is a true, sometimes indescribable, inner peace that comes once you genuinely understand who created you, who created all living things. You will know the one who holds the future. And you will know the one who can make your life significant.

MORE REFLECTION:

- "Listen to me, O house of Jacob, all you who remain of the house of Israel, you whom I have upheld since you were conceived and have carried since your birth. Even to your old age and gray hairs I am he, I am he who will sustain you. I have made you and I will carry you; I will sustain you and I will rescue you" (Isaiah 46:3-4).
- "Listen to me, you islands; hear this, you distant nations: Before I was born the Lord called me; from my birth he has made mention of my name" (Isaiah 49:1).

FOR PONDERING FURTHER:

1. According to this verse, when does life begin?
2. When did your relationship with God start?
3. What do you think about that?
4. How does this affect what you see as your purpose in life?

LAST THOUGHT:

REST IN THE TRUTH THAT GOD CREATED YOU FOR A REASON.

FORTY-ONE

The Applause of Heaven

Not to us, O Lord, not to us but to your name be the glory, because of your love and faithfulness.
Psalms 115:1

Whether it's a pro football player doing a ridiculous dance after an incredible touchdown or a high school basketball star gloating for a week after hitting the game-winning shot, it's likely you're accustomed to seeing someone celebrating when his performance is outstanding.

"LOOK AT ME!" their actions shout. "I DID SOMETHING WORTH NOTICING!" It's not just the attention they want. They want the credit, if only for a few brief seconds.

We all need attention—especially in childhood. Kids will come (or at least look) to mom and dad after coloring a cool picture, getting good grades, building an elaborate Lincoln log house—or accomplishing a thousand other "feats." Parents can't help but go ga-ga over their child's achievements, and no child can resist his parents' praise.

In reality, we all need positive feedback after a job well done. And at home, we like to hear thank you's and other words of appreciation for even the small stuff.

With seven billion people on the planet, most of us want to avoid becoming simply another nameless face in the crowd. Many of us wouldn't mind being famous for a while. To be set above the rest gives us a measure of pride in knowing we're not wallowing with the masses in obscurity. It's normal to want to be noticed by a newspaper photographer or reporter. To be praised or highly esteemed by peers—even strangers—somehow means you're being recognized for hard work, a special ability, or an unusual feat of excellence.

To WANT recognition is normal, but to LIVE for it is spiritually dangerous. And the line between the two isn't that wide. Stage actors are said to be addicted to the applause from those who come to see them perform. Many of them are devastated if adoration or positive reviews don't accompany their hard work on stage. When they don't get the praise their reason for living has been wiped away and they feel worthless.

The psalmist knew the dangers that accompany the praise of men, and he was aware that the only way to avoid the snare of LIVING to receive the credit—the glory—was to deflect it toward God. When a football player kneels in the end zone after scoring a touchdown, many (though probably not all) are communicating to the Lord their gratefulness. When a baseball player gets on camera after hitting the game-winning homer and the first words out of his mouth are, "First of all, I want to thank my Lord and Savior, Jesus Christ..." he's fought the urge to take all the credit for his accomplishment.

Are you thankful for the abilities God gave you—enough to appropriately and with true humility deflect the praise in the right direction?

A few people in life's journey will receive the applause of the crowd, but most of us will hear only some thanks for a job well done. Both are unpredictable and last for only a moment. LIVING for either leads to a sad existence.

Your ego doesn't need to be so fragile as to constantly seek the approval of man. God, by sending Jesus, has already shown His approval of you. For that, He deserves whatever earthly praise you receive in life. His love and faithfulness are truly a higher reward than any glory you could ever attain.

It's OK to say "Thanks" when you're congratulated, but remember . . . it's your heart God is most concerned with. From deep within, you can deflect the praise of men back to God without saying a word. When you do this, you get something back that you can't hear: the applause of heaven.

MORE REFLECTION:

- "For, as I have often told you before and now say again even with tears, many live as enemies of the cross of Christ. Their destiny is destruction, their god is their stomach, and their glory is in their shame. Their mind is on earthly things. But our citizenship is in heaven" (Philippians 3:18-20a).
- "The fear of the Lord teaches a man wisdom, and humility comes before honor" (Proverbs 16:33).

FOR PONDERING FURTHER:

1. What do you receive the most praise for in your life?

2. How does it make you feel when everyone's attention is drawn to you?
3. Could you get used to it? Do you have it within you to LIVE for it?
4. If you never heard another word of praise in your life, but knew how much God loves you, could you live with that?

LAST THOUGHT:
TRY DEFLECTING THE PRAISE YOU RECEIVE BACK TO GOD.

FORTY-TWO

The Unavoidable Subject

*Even though I walk through the valley of
the shadow of death,
I will fear no evil, for you are with me;
your rod and your staff,
they comfort me.*
Psalms 23:4

Steve's life was a blast in every way. He had friends, a car, pocket cash from his job at a shoe store, his own room, an I-phone 6s, mom, dad, grandma, grandpa—life was great. Then in his junior year of high school, his dad had a sudden heart attack. He died two weeks later.

No longer would he and his dad shoot hoops together, play tennis, or laugh together while watching dumb movies. Life would forever be different. Within a short period of time, Steve wasn't a kid who could do most anything he wanted. Now he was the man of the house.

As a Christian, Steve knew he'd see his dad again. That wasn't the issue. The issue was that life was no longer constant fun. He had to grow up sooner than he wanted. It was tough for Steve, but after a few months he adjusted to this new role and freely admitted to his youth group that he was a better person than he was before. Death had taught him some things about life he'd never considered before.

Most people feel invincible. They think they'll escape death until they're too old to care. Teenagers are especially notorious for believing that death only happens to *other* people.

It's never pleasant to be confronted with death. But there are some things you can learn from the concept. Let's make a list:

- *It will give you an appreciation for YOUR life.* Since life is essentially your only experience, it's the best game in town. You should learn to savor each day as a gift.
- *It will help you appreciate the lives of OTHERS.* It's easy to take the people God has placed around you for granted. To truly enjoy and appreciate them, you must look at them through different eyes. There will be a time when you won't see this person in this world again. You should be more thankful to have the chance to be with them another day.
- *It might make you realize you need a bridge to the next life.* God and your parents gave you a bridge to this life, but only God can give you a bridge to the next. What is that bridge? Jesus Christ, of course. The moment you slip from earth life to eternal life, he will be there to take your hand and escort you to the Father.
- *It may remind you of the Good Shepherd, who loves you.* What was David talking about when he said God's rod and staff were *comforting?* David knew something about the shepherd heart of God. He knew what it meant to have the Lord as his Shepherd: when it was time to move to a different pasture,

God could be trusted to lead him to the safety and security of a better place than before.
- *After facing death, it will be easier to face any challenge that comes along.* Once you realize God is with you in the deep valley of what you perceive as "the worst of the worst" possible events, no event or challenge is too great. If God can walk with you through death, He can walk with you in new school hallways, in college, in the big game, in marriage . . . ANYWHERE!

Death needs to be thoughtfully considered in order to refocus your heart on what is important in life. Perhaps the greatest lesson of this verse are those four little words, "you are with me."

MORE REFLECTION:
- "This is the day the Lord has made; let us rejoice and be glad in it" (Psalms 118:24).
- "Teach us to number our days aright, that we may gain a heart of wisdom" (Psalms 90:12).

FOR PONDERING FURTHER:
1. Short of death, what are some things you would consider to be bad if they happened to you?
2. Do you fear the "evil" things that could happen to you?
3. On a scale of 1 to 10, how trusting are you in God?
4. Why do you think that most teens avoid the subject of death?

LAST THOUGHT:
FOCUS ON WHAT IS IMPORTANT IN THIS LIFE.

FORTY-THREE

Waiting for Deliverance

The Lord is close to the brokenhearted and saves those who are crushed in spirit. A righteous man may have many troubles, but the Lord delivers him from them all.
Psalms 34:18-19

A couple of years after Steve's father died, he talked about the times late at night when the pain of never seeing him again in this life was deeper than any pain he had ever felt. He talked about how he would pray for God to take the pain away. He desperately wanted to be delivered from his broken-heartedness.

Until you are faced with something like the death of someone you love (see previous meditation), it's tough to pray for deliverance with too much seriousness. When people say, "Lord deliver me," it's often more of a faithless plea to escape an annoying circumstance than a prayer for deliverance.

But one day—or perhaps many days—you'll say those words and really mean them. It won't be for an exam you didn't study for or a parental decision you don't agree with. It will be much worse. Your spirit will be crushed because something awful has happened to you or a loved one. God will be the only place to turn.

Most of us would add the word *immediately* right after *Lord* and before *deliver*, as in "Lord, *immediately* deliver me!" But that word is missing, isn't it? Any guesses as to why? Did God accidentally leave it out? Or is it implied that He WILL deliver immediately, so He didn't need to put it in? Or was it left out on purpose? Does God delay deliverance until it's absolutely necessary?

Occasionally, God will deliver immediately. But more often, He waits for the right time. "Never early, never late," is a motto God could easily take as His own.

How do you feel about that? Can you trust God enough to allow him to deliver you when HE wants, instead of when YOU want?

And what if He brought deliverance in a way you didn't anticipate? What if deliverance came weeks after you thought it was needed, and the way you were delivered was simply by time doing its magic and making the hurt go away?

The biggest issue these questions raise is: Can God be trusted to be God?

The answer, of course, is yes. Millions of people trust God every day. They've learned that trouble often comes, and that a crushed spirit is sometimes unavoidable. But instead of seeking their own solutions, they patiently rely on a loving God to help them through their pain. They know that even a righteous person has troubles, but that the Lord delivers them from them all—eventually.

MORE REFLECTION:

- "Praise be to the Lord, to God our Savior, who daily bears our burdens. Our God is a God who saves; from the Sovereign Lord comes escape from death" (Psalms 68:19-20).
- "God is our refuge and strength, an ever-present help in trouble. Therefore we will not fear, though the earth give and the mountains fall into the heart of the sea, though its waters roar and foam and the mountains quake with their surging" (Psalms 46:1-3).

FOR PONDERING FURTHER:

1. Has anything ever broken your heart?
2. Do you think you could trust God enough to allow Him to deliver you in H*is* time?
3. What types of troubles do you experience now?
4. How do you think the Lord stays close to the brokenhearted and those who are going through troubles?

LAST THOUGHT:
WE MUST TRUST GOD DURING TIMES OF ANGUISH.

FORTY-FOUR

Conditional Promises

*Delight yourself in the Lord and he will
give you the desires of your heart.*
Psalms 37:4

A condition, a promise. Did you see it in this verse? Most people skip right by the condition and concentrate on the promise.

"Delight yourself in the Lord" is the condition, and "he will give you the desires of your heart" is the promise.

Do you ever get conditional promises and privileges at home? Of course you do. Probably all the time. "Keep your grades up, and you can use the car." "Do your chores, and you can stay out that extra hour on Friday night."

Not ALL promises God gives have conditions (nor do all promises your parents give), but many do. Taking apart this verse will yield some clues on what it means.

Delight implies enjoyment. It means giving attention to, even loving. It's the choice you make that God truly longs for. He wants you to be more excited for Him than when you are when you can't wait to do something like watch a TV show, go to a basketball game, or go out on a date.

When you have genuine delight in spending time with Him, He offers an incredible promise: the desires of your heart. Not the lusts, not the greeds, but your deep-down—righteous—desires. But don't think that God will *immediately* grant you the desires of your heart. God is not like the attendant at a drive-thru window at McDonald's, who gives you your order in minutes. *True* desires are typically big things that demand patience for them to be fulfilled. Things such as:

- A life mate
- A career
- Seeing a loved one come to know the Lord

Big stuff, true. But they demand the supernatural intervention of the Lord if they are going to happen in the right way and at the right time. Truthfully, they're the type of desires you can't conjure up yourself. God plants them within you. When that happens, your desires have become His desires.

Learning to delight yourself in the invisible God doesn't happen overnight, either. In fact, it is a lifetime process. Just as the love between a married couple matures through the decades, so will your love and delight for God. He knows what you're capable of at fifteen and understands that the depth of that delight will be different when you're twenty-five. So He'll take what you have today, knowing that tomorrow can be even better. All the while He's cherishing those thoughts of delight you have for Him and preparing to fulfill His end of the bargain: the desires of your heart.

MORE REFLECTION:

- "Let us hold unswervingly to the hope we profess, for he who promised is faithful" (Hebrews 10:23).
- "He will keep you strong to the end, so that you will be blameless on the day of our Lord Jesus Christ. God, who has

called you into fellowship with his son Jesus Christ our Lord, is faithful" (1 Corinthians 1:8-9).

FOR PONDERING FURTHER:
1. What does it mean to "delight" yourself in someone?
2. Have you ever done that before?
3. What *are* the deep-down desires of your heart?
4. What *should* be the deep-down desires of your heart?

LAST THOUGHT:
LEARN TO DELIGHT YOURSELF IN THE LORD.

FORTY-FIVE

Moving to the Next Level

I have set the Lord always before me. Because he is at my right hand, I will not be shaken.
Psalms 16:8

You have probably heard many times that daily devotions are really important if you want to grow as a Christian. But unless you're a disciplined machine, you're likely a bit frustrated by your lack of accomplishing regular Bible reading and prayer.

It's true that consistency is important. And, yes, a daily time to connect with God really CAN help keep you relationally on track with Him. But what are His expectations? What does H*e* want from you on a daily basis? A structured fifteen minutes? Or does He want more?

Here's the truth: God wants more than five minutes, or twenty . . . or an hour. He wants it all. He wants you to get to the point where you're communicating with Him all day. Since He's by your side every minute—guiding, protecting, listening, speaking—He'd like it if you kept in better touch with Him.

Communicating with God throughout your day takes practice. If you'd like to increase your awareness of God you can try some of these visible reminders:

A few words written on your notebook: "I'm here." "Remember me?" "You're not alone!" "Talk to me." It doesn't have to be obtrusive or overtly fanatic. Most of your friends won't know what it means... but you'll know, and that's the idea.

A friend or two to help you refocus. Perhaps there's a couple of Christians at your school who are ready to move to this level of communion with God. In the hallway between classes, at lunch, a phone call on the weekends—wherever you can, whatever it takes—you can subtly remind each other to remember the Lord. Perhaps "Remember the Lord" becomes the phrase you use. That's all you'll have to say.

Being a Christian isn't simply following a set of moral guidelines, going to church, knowing the right "Christianese," or reading your Bible for a few minutes a day. The fun part is realizing God wants you to know He's around all day—every day—and that he desires constant communication. When you're ready to move to the next level and set Him before you at all times, He's ready, too.

MORE REFLECTION:

- "Pray continually..." (1 Thessalonians 5:17).
- "And pray in the Spirit on all occasions with all kinds of prayers and requests. With this in mind, be alert and always keep on praying for all the saints" (Ephesians 6:18).

FOR PONDERING FURTHER:

1. Do you ever get weary of trying to maintain a time of "daily devotions"?

2. Does communicating with God dozens of times a day seem possible?
3. What holds you back: desire or reminders?
4. Do you know someone who would help you remember the Lord?

LAST THOUGHT:
TRY TO MAKE THE LORD MORE OF A PART OF YOUR DAY.

FORTY-SIX

The Loneliness Solution

Turn to me and be gracious to me, for I am lonely and afflicted. The troubles of my heart have multiplied; free me from my anguish.
Psalms 25:16-17

Not all loneliness is bad. In fact, it can be a positive. For instance:

- You can be reminded of your unseen companion who, whether you recognize it or not, is constantly by your side.
- It can give you moments to do some reflecting on the direction your life is taking.
- You may realize that books can become a healthy escape. Reading great fiction or biographies about the lives of others long ago can allow you to make "friends" with people you can learn from and relate to.
- Perhaps your loneliness will draw you to someone who truly needs a friend, just like you.

But loneliness can also be unbearable. Some people allow their loneliness to push them to a sense of hopelessness.

The apostle Paul, the great missionary who wrote about half of the New Testament (everything from Romans to Philemon), tasted loneliness more than most. Read this passage carefully and try to imagine how you would have felt had you experienced all that he did.

> *I have worked much harder, been in prison more frequently, been flogged more severely, and been exposed to death again and again. Five times I received from the Jews the forty lashes minus one. Three times I was beaten with rods, once I was stoned, three times I was shipwrecked, I spent a night and a day in the open sea, I have been constantly on the move. I have been in danger from rivers, in danger from bandits, in danger from my own countrymen, in danger from Gentiles; in danger in the city, in danger in country, in danger at sea; and in danger from false brothers. I have labored and toiled and have often gone without sleep; I have known hunger and thirst and have often gone without food; I have been cold and naked. Besides everything else, I face daily the pressure of my concern for all the churches* (2 Corinthians 11:23-28).

All of this, and Paul still had another ten years to live before he was beheaded by a Roman sword. How could he live without giving up in the face of incredible persecution . . . and times when he must have felt all alone?

First, he knew he wasn't truly alone. Second, he had a mission that was bigger than his own life. He had something to live for. His loneliness never led to feelings of hopelessness.

The ultimate solution for loneliness isn't just a friend, but having something to live for, something so important to do that waking up in the morning is a privilege, not a dreaded chore. Sooner or later, someone who does not have a mission in life, something that gives life purpose, will know true loneliness—and hopelessness. Noise, things, pleasures, and other distractions can only deaden the loneliness, not take it away. Freedom from inevitable anguish is found in knowing who made you, who's with you, and why He gave you life.

MORE REFLECTION:

- (Paul talking, in his last letter before he was executed) "At my first defense, no one came to my support, but everyone deserted me. May it not be held against them. But the Lord stood at my side and gave me strength, so that through me the message might be fully proclaimed and all the Gentiles might hear it. And I was delivered from the lion's mouth. The Lord will rescue me from every evil attack and will bring me safely to his heavenly kingdom" (2 Timothy 4:16-18a).
- "Then the Jews came from Antioch and Iconium and won the crowd over. They stoned Paul and dragged him outside the city, thinking he was dead. But after the disciples had gathered around him, he got up and went back into the city. The next day he and Barnabas left for Derbe. They preached the good news in that city and won a large number of disciples. Then they returned to Lystra, Iconium and Antioch, strengthening the disciples and encouraging them to remain true to the faith. 'We must go through many hardships to enter the kingdom of God,' they said" (Acts 14:19-22).

FOR PONDERING FURTHER:

1. When do you feel most lonely?
2. What do you do when that feeling hits?
3. How can reaching out to other people help cure your loneliness?
4. How have people reached out to you when you've been lonely?

LAST THOUGHT:

PURSUE THE MISSION GOD HAS GIVEN YOU.

FORTY-SEVEN

Does God Make Mistakes in Judgment?

He will judge the world in righteousness;
he will govern the peoples with justice. The
Lord is a refuge for the oppressed, a
stronghold in times of trouble.
Psalms 9:8-9

When it looks as if someone in class is cheating on a test, the teacher has a few choices. She can . . .
1. Wait until class is over and confront the student.
2. Walk up to the student's desk and tear up the paper in front of everyone.
3. Do nothing, knowing that for every cheater caught, five more get away with it.

It's a tough choice for the teacher. What if the student really *wasn't* cheating? What if it was the first time he *ever* looked at another student's paper? Does he really deserve the shame?

What's the *just* thing to do? If you were the teacher who had to make the decision, what would you do? Confront and convict? Discuss it after class? Or do nothing?

We don't use the words *judge* or *justice* too often, but most of us know when judgments are wrong and when justice *hasn't* been served. And we don't like it when that happens. Neither does God.

In several places, the Bible mentions God's judgment, as well as His desire for justice. If we were honest, most of us would admit that we'd rather have justice without judgment. But you can't separate the two, and that's the part of God's character that worries many believers. But this passage is saying, "Don't worry. He'll do it right."

God's process for making a final judgment isn't what most people think. It's true that God is a judge—but He's a lot more. He's not only judge, He's also a prosecuting attorney! That's right, He's the one who knows everything about us . . . and convicts us. He tells it like it is—our heart is wicked and deceitful above all else. But He doesn't just play judge and prosecuting attorney. He's also our defense attorney.

"Yes, your Honor," Jesus says, "these people you have created *are* guilty. They inherited their sin from Adam. They deserve death. But I know your character. You're a good judge, and it's not your desire to punish someone you've so lovingly created. Can't you find another way to satisfy your anger over their sin and disobedient nature?"

A careful examination of Scripture will show you that God granted the defense attorney's request. The Judge asked him—Jesus—to step in the place of all humanity and receive the sentence of death. "You taste spiritual death for them," God said.

His only Son said, "I will."

God is judge, prosecuting attorney, defense attorney . . . and the condemned victim, all at the same time.

That's why you can wholeheartedly believe this passage when it says, "He will judge the world in righteousness; he will govern the people with justice." He will make no mistakes in His judgment—with you or anyone else.

MORE REFLECTION:

- "So we say with confidence, 'The Lord is my helper; I will not be afraid. What can man do to me?'" (Hebrews 13:6).
- "As for the person who hears my words but does not keep them, I do not judge him. For I did not come to judge the world, but to save it. There is a judge for the one who rejects me and does not accept my words; that very word which I spoke will condemn him at the last day" (John 12:47-48).

FOR PONDERING FURTHER:

1. What do you think it means when God is described as a fair judge?
2. Have you ever been judged unfairly by a parent or a friend? How did you feel?
3. Have you ever made a mistake in judging someone else? How did you feel when you found out the truth?

LAST THOUGHT:

REST ASSURED THAT GOD WILL NOT MAKE ANY MISTAKES IN HIS JUDGMENT OF THE WORLD.

FORTY-EIGHT

Looking Through the Right End of the Telescope

*I will remember the deeds of the Lord; yes,
I will remember your miracles of long ago.
I will meditate on all your works
and consider all your mighty deeds.*
Psalms 77:11-12

"What have you done for me lately?"

Not many have the gall to actually say those words to a parent, grandparent, or friend. But many people have this attitude. They only want to remember recent events.

David made a commitment to remember all that God had done for him. He chose *not* to have spiritual "selective memory."

It takes work to think on the past. The reason? It's easy—even natural—to focus on the present or the near future. After all, that's where you live. But failing to reflect on the good things from the past breeds ungratefulness, a bad habit to get into.

Many parents—perhaps your own—will freely admit they didn't start appreciating their own mother and father until they began having kids themselves. Then they finally realized all their folks went through, all they sacrificed. That means their parents may have had to wait twenty-five or thirty years before they received a genuine, "Wow, I didn't realize all you had to go through. Thanks for what you did for me these past twenty-five years." Better late than never, true. But how sad for the parent who willingly gives up personal dreams and pleasures to care for children, then must wait a quarter of a century to hear words of appreciation.

Sadly, it happens all the time between parent and child. But even more disappointing, it happens all the time between the Christian and God. Again, it's not often stated, perhaps not intentional, but a believer's behavior often points to that selfishness disease: "What have you done for me lately, God?"

The cure, David discovered, was meditating on what God had done in the past, actually sitting down, getting quiet, and thinking. Suddenly realizing what God has done for you can make the present and the future seem bright. What has God done for you?

He's provided parents, a roof, bed, pillow, stuff in your room, clothes, and food. He's given you grandparents who send gifts, even when they don't receive a thank-you note for three years in a row. He's given you friends.

A God who loved you enough to die in your place.

When you commit to remembering what God has done, you will strengthen your faith.

MORE REFLECTION:

- "Remember your Creator in the days of your youth, before the days of trouble come and the years approach when you will say, 'I find no pleasure in them'" (Ecclesiastes 12:1).
- "When times are good, be happy; but when times are bad, consider: God has made the one as well as the other" (Ecclesiastes 7:14).

FOR PONDERING FURTHER:

1. Can you remember any specific things your parents have done for you in the past? What were they?
2. How about things God has done for you?
3. Why do you think David wanted to remember the deeds of the Lord?
4. How can looking at God's faithfulness to people in the Bible give you comfort today?

LAST THOUGHT:

REMEMBER ALL THAT GOD HAS DONE FOR YOU.

FORTY-NINE

More than Words

I have hidden your word in my heart
that I might not sin against you....
I meditate on your precepts
and consider your ways.
I delight in your decrees;
I will not neglect your word.
Psalms 119:11, 15-16

Few things are more important in the Christian life than loving God's Word, knowing God's Word, and giving consistent attention to God's Word.

The Bible isn't just another book. If you've got it stuck in your brain that its words aren't any different than those of a novel or a textbook, the Bible will get old... really fast. But if you knew for certain that when you read the Bible, you were actually spending time with Jesus, your reading habits would change. If you're not usually an avid reader, what would motivate you more: reading a book or being with a person?

John 1 refers to Jesus as "the Word of God." Hebrews 4:12 says the Bible is "living and active." These and many other passages confirm that when you read the Bible you're not just spending time with black-and-white type; you're investing a few minutes with Jesus.

The Bible is not just a collection of sterile stories about a bunch of dead guys. It contains the most important things God wanted to say to His creation. No, not every word is going to relate to you during your teenage years. This is obvious if you've ever read through Leviticus. But don't forget, God has been trying to relate to teenagers through His written Word for 3,000 years. He's also had the huge task of communicating His character and plan to adults in all stages of life for the past thirty centuries. The pressures and problems, the lifestyles and cultures have been vastly different during that time, yet a high percentage of the words in the Bible have been a source of comfort, strength, and guidance for all who give them attention.

If you approach the Bible as if you were actually spending time with the same Jesus who died and rose again, get ready to truly know and love the God of the Bible.

MORE REFLECTION:

- "Your word is a lamp to my feet and a light for my path" (Psalms 119:105).
- "As the deer pants for streams of water, so my soul pants for you, O God. My soul thirsts for God, for the living God. When can I go and meet with God?" (Psalms 42:1-2).

FOR PONDERING FURTHER:

1. What does it take to motivate you to spend time in the Bible?
2. What goes through your mind when you read it?
3. Would believing you were spending time with a person instead of a book help you to get into it a little more?

4. How could a friend or parent help you to read the Bible a little more often?

LAST THOUGHT:
SPENDING TIME IN THE BIBLE IS SPENDING TIME WITH JESUS CHRIST.

FIFTY

The Freedom to Go

*So I gave them over to their stubborn hearts
to follow their own devices.*
Psalms 81:22

God is persistent, but He has a breaking point. No, He doesn't "give up" on anyone, but occasionally, the time arrives when God allows those who want to retain control of their lives to do so. Like the father in the story of the Prodigal Son (see Luke 15), God knows when arguments won't work, when the heart and mind are set on steering a different course, and when no amount of words can move the life's rudder of His child.

That's when God does something that must break His heart. He gives His child over to His or Her own stubborn ways. It's not the childish response of, "Fine, just go. I don't care." It's an anguished resignation of, "Well, I'd hoped it would never come to this. But I love you enough not to control you. Go if you must."

If you recall that story of the Prodigal, the son takes his dad's cash and heads off to the big city to do whatever his heart desires. Soon, his money and "friends" are gone . . . and he's feeding pigs to stay alive!

Have you ever thought about what the father was doing while his son was having his fill of a stubborn heart? He was waiting. But it wasn't the kind of waiting that has an "I told you so" verbal volley ready to fire the moment his "evil" son walked in the front door. It was the kind of waiting a stubborn heart truly needs: a knowing and an anticipation that the father would accept him back—on any terms. It was hope that there might be a future together with him again. And, most importantly, it was a waiting with grace and forgiveness—perhaps even a little forgetfulness.

The son was not disappointed. Though he had been given over to pursue the "freedom" he felt he needed, he never heard an "I told you so" (at least not from the father). Dad was just glad to have his son back. We're not told of the consequences he had to face, if any. Maybe the memory of having disappointed and hurt so many people was enough.

Some young adults seem destined to be a prodigal. They want to cut their own path in life, and aren't sure of—or don't want—God's involvement. If you believe you may have that bent, be assured of four things:

1. God WILL give you over if you choose to leave His protection.
2. You WILL eventually "feed pigs" as a result (in this life or the next). And it won't be pleasant.
3. God WILL be hoping, waiting for you to return.
4. He WILL give you the exact type of homecoming you need so you can see His true character.

Unfortunately, some people must learn the hard way. Which will you choose?

MORE REFLECTION:

- "For although they knew God, they neither glorified him as God nor gave thanks to him, but their thinking became futile and their foolish hearts were darkened. Although they claimed to be wise, they became fools and exchanged the glory of the immortal God for images made to look like mortal man and birds and animals and reptiles. Therefore God gave them over to the sinful desires of their hearts..." (Romans 1:21-24).

- "Or do you show contempt for the riches of his kindness, tolerance, and patience, not realizing that God's kindness leads you toward repentance? But because of your stubbornness and your unrepentant heart, you are storing up wrath against yourself for the day of God's wrath, when his righteous judgment will be revealed" (Romans 2:4-5).

FOR PONDERING FURTHER:

1. Why do you think God would give anyone over to a stubborn heart?
2. What do you think that looks like?
3. Can you learn from others' mistakes, or do you need to make your own?
4. Are you perceptive enough to envision potential consequences to your actions? Or do you act first, then face the music later?

LAST THOUGHT:
GOD WELCOMES BACK THE PRODIGAL WHO CHOOSES TO RETURN TO HIM.

FIFTY-ONE

Under Control

*In your anger do not sin; when you are on
your beds, search your hearts and be silent.*
Psalms 4:4

An annoying little sister. A bullying big brother. A parent who won't ever let you explain your side. A friend who never calls when she says she will. A teacher who gives tons of homework on Fridays. That elderly driver who cut you off on the freeway and didn't even care.

Life's daily irritations can make you hit red on the "anger meter." But this verse says not to get angry. So when you do, you're sinning, right? Wrong! Read it again.

The verse assumes you're going to get angry. Why? Because anger, like love, is a natural emotion. Something that starts inside your brain. It's even needed at times . . . when it's under control.

Uncontrolled laughter is fun to watch, but uncontrolled anger is not. Whether it's prolonged yelling and screaming, swearing, or physical contact, when played out by someone with no self-control, anger is ugly (not to mention dangerous). The reason: uncontrolled anger breeds hurt feelings, unforgiveness, resentment, and hate.

Here are several other problems with uncontrolled anger:
- *It's everywhere.* Most humans have a temper, and when it reaches a certain level, it bursts out like a leak in a dam.
- *It's allowed.* You probably know several friends or relatives who get angry fairly often. Most likely, these people are never confronted about how they play out their anger. (Why? Because they'll get angry!).
- *It's progressive.* If not checked, the angry person eventually learns to get angrier. If a little anger accomplishes what they want, a LOT of anger will get even more.
- *It's destructive.* Relationships are ruined by the long-term effects of anger. And the angry person would be in for internal health problems because of that anger.

Anger is usually about *being in control.* When you can't control the circumstances or behavior of something or someone, you get angry. Look over the examples mentioned in the first paragraph. If you could control each of those problems, you wouldn't get angry, right?

People who are consistently angry are often insecure. They don't like who they are, so in order to feel good about themselves, they have to control everyone around them. When they're not in control, they explode until they regain that control.

Enough of the negative. What are the potential benefits of anger?
- *Seeing injustice at your school* (sticking up for a kid who is always picked on) *or in the world* (ethnic prejudices) could make you angry to the point of wanting to right the wrong.
- *Getting angry at your own consistent sin patterns* can motivate you to do all it takes to rid yourself of them.

David discovered what it takes to *use* your anger instead of *being used* by it: "... search your hearts and be silent." In other words, think about what makes you boil, trace it to its source (or ask someone else to help you trace it), then act on your anger for good.

MORE REFLECTION:

- "Do not make friends with a hot-tempered man, do not associate with one easily angered, or you may learn his ways and get yourself ensnared" (Proverbs 22:24-25).
- "My dear brothers, take note of this: Everyone should be quick to listen, slow to speak and slow to become angry, for man's anger does not bring about the righteous life that God desires" (James 1:19-20).

FOR PONDERING FURTHER:

1. What makes you *really* angry?
2. How do you normally vent your anger?
3. Has it ever gotten you into trouble?
4. When have you used your anger to accomplish something good?

LAST THOUGHT:

WORK TO CONTROL YOUR ANGER, RATHER THAN ALLOWING IT TO CONTROL *YOU*.

FIFT-TWO

A Heart Undivided

*Teach me your way, O Lord, and I will
walk in your truth; give me an undivided
heart, that I may fear your name.*
Psalms 86:11

Those two words tucked near the middle of this verse—*undivided heart*—are easy to miss, but they are very important.

What is an undivided heart? Crassly put, it's a heart that isn't chopped to pieces and spread out all over the place.

Can you have a divided heart toward education and expect to get into a good college? Not unless you're a natural genius.

If you had a divided heart when it came to doing well in a varsity sport, would you play much or get a scholarship? Probably not.

A divided heart in a relationship with the opposite sex will most likely get you a very brief stint together.

In short, if you want to *get by* you can have a divided heart and still do some of what you want to do. The only way to win with God, according to David, was to give it everything you've got. Close doesn't count in following God.

It's not heaven a divided-heart believer will miss out on; it's what God could have done through you here on earth. The real tragedy is the realization—at some point in your existence—*of what could have been.*

Maintaining an undivided heart means keeping all the pieces together. How do you do that? David gave two hints in this verse alone.

- *Staying teachable.* David is still saying, "Teach me your way." While we don't know his age, it's safe to assume he wasn't a young buck anymore. Whether he was thirty or forty, this passage implies he didn't know it all. He needed to know more. Why? So he could walk in the truth.
- *Fearing the Lord.* The word *fear* actually means to "revere." To have reverence for God's name is the ultimate form of respect. That's one reason why you're not to take God's name in vain—you're not showing respect. Failing to respect God means you don't believe there is another ruler besides yourself. In essence, your heart is divided over who sits on the throne, who's in control. When this is the case, you're settling for second best.

The scriptures are filled with other ways to maintain an undivided heart: prayer, fellowship, worship, serving others, saying no to temptation, giving your money away. If an undivided heart is your goal, ask God to teach you His truth so your heart will always stay in one piece.

MORE REFLECTION:

- "Devote yourselves to prayer, being watchful and thankful" (Colossians 4:2).

- "Jesus knew their thoughts and said to them: 'Any kingdom divided against itself will be ruined, and a house divided against itself will fall'" (Luke 11:17).

FOR PONDERING FURTHER:

1. What would keep you from completely surrendering your heart to God?
2. What is an "undivided heart?" How would you describe your heart?
3. If you wholeheartedly served God, what would that do to your ministry at school?

LAST THOUGHT:
KEEP YOUR HEART WHOLLY DEVOTED TO GOD.

FIFTY-THREE

He's God, and You're Not

*I will declare your name to my brothers; in
the congregation I will praise you.*
Psalms 22:22

Let's face it, God is bored and insecure. He sits up in heaven with a bunch of angels who use out-of-tune harps to play melodies He's heard a million times already. He's tired of it, so He told a few men on earth to write down that it's important to praise him. At least that way, He'd get a little more variety, a little attention . . . and get a few strokes for His weak ego. After all, He's God—and His puny creation isn't!

Sometimes you have to say it wrong to get it right. And the previous paragraph was mostly wrong. Except that last sentence (but let's take out the word puny).

He's God and I'm not.

Hmmmmmm.

Do you like the sound of that? Some do, but most don't.

Most people are adamant about staying in control: "It's my life, so I'll do with it whatever I want." When God hears that from your lips or sees that attitude within your heart (He can do both, you know), He doesn't scream and yell and call you an idiot. He lets you take control. You see, He's not pushy and He's definitely not a control freak. Not that He doesn't want control. He does because He knows that if He's allowed control, your life will be far more excellent than you could ever make it if you kept your hands on the buttons.

He knows it. You know it. But even Christians will struggle with control. (It's that sin disease thing again.)

Enter, stage right . . . praise.

If only for a moment, praising God takes your focus off the buttons you want to push and says, "You alone are the Master button pusher. Take the control panel of my life and push the right buttons." (Most likely, this line will never appear in a hymn book . . . or even on a K-Love play list.)

You've heard before, "It's the thought that counts." And God wants your thoughts off yourself and on Him so He *can* push the right buttons.

Praise allows Him to do that.

Twenty minutes of praise a week isn't enough. Twenty *hours* probably isn't, either. But however you do it, praising Him is good for you.

There are many ways you can praise God. When you serve others, give away your money, sing, pray, and read your Bible, you're communicating to God exactly what He knows you need to say: "You're God, and I'm not."

MORE REFLECTION:

- "I do not hide your righteousness in my heart; I speak of your faithfulness and salvation. I do not conceal your love and your truth from the great assembly" (Psalms 40:10).
- "At that time Jesus said, 'I praise you, Father, Lord of heaven and earth, because you have hidden these things from the wise and learned and revealed them to little children. Yes, Father, for this was your good pleasure'" (Matthew 11:25-26).

FOR PONDERING FURTHER:

1. What is your opinion about singing praises to God?
2. Why do we need to praise Him?
3. Why is that difficult to do?
4. What other ways can you praise God besides singing?

LAST THOUGHT:

TRY PRAISING GOD MORE OFTEN, RECOGNIZING THAT HE'S GOD AND YOU'RE NOT.

FIFTY-FOUR

Clean Slate Freedom

Blessed is he whose transgressions are forgiven, whose sins are covered. Blessed is the man whose sin the Lord does not count against him and in whose spirit is no deceit.
Psalms 31:102

There is something almost magical about having the slate wiped clean, about beginning anew.

- *A new term* with a new teacher means the grade book is empty, and once again you have the opportunity to start over.
- *A new job* means your boss is not going to judge you by the mistake you made the week before.
- When you start practice for *a new basketball season with a new coach,* there are no prejudices from previous years, so you have as good of a chance to make the team as anyone else.
- *New Year's Day* is a day when the previous year can be (semi-) forgotten.

What if you could start anew each day? As a Christian, of course, you can. The bricks of sin that form a wall between you and God can be torn down and thrown away. A close, open relationship with Him is achieved the moment you confess your sins and humbly ask God to forgive you. The slate is supernaturally erased.

Too often, however, Christian teens let the bricks accumulate between them and God. What kind of bricks? Cheating on a test, watching some internet videos you know you shouldn't, letting a few swear words slip, lying, showing disrespect for their parents, allowing impure thoughts to go unchecked. You know, sin bricks.

Unconfessed sin over a long period of time makes it tough to admit to God what He already knows . . . but what you need to say to Him.

Why is confession of sin to God so tough when you haven't done it for a while?

After a long time of neglect, the brick wall makes you feel as if God is far away, as if your prayers are bouncing off the ceiling. Sadly, some don't believe it's enough to ask for forgiveness after neglecting to do it for so long. The reason: they aren't sure He would actually wipe the slate clean in a few minutes of humble confession. And though admitting to God what He already knows *does* tear the wall down, they don't *feel* like it's gone.

But it is! Completely! That's why David calls you "blessed" when your transgressions have been forgiven. The slate *is* clean. Though you may feel you cannot look God in the eye and know your sins have been wiped away, God reaffirms over and over in His Word that this is the case.

A brand new day to start fresh.

You again become blessed.

Know it. Feel it. Count on it.

MORE REFLECTION:

- "'Come now, let us reason together,' says the Lord. 'Though your sins are like scarlet, they shall be as white as snow; though they are red as crimson, they shall be like wool'" (Isaiah 1:18).
- "If we confess our sins, he is faithful and just and will forgive us our sins and purify us from all unrighteousness" (1 John 1:9).

FOR PONDERING FURTHER:

1. How would you feel if a teacher judged you by the last year's performance?
2. If a parent always reminded you about past failures, would you ever feel truly forgiven?
3. When someone in your life wipes the slate completely clean, what are your feelings toward them?
4. How does God wipe the slate clean in your life?

LAST THOUGHT:

GOD IS ALWAYS READY TO WIPE THE SLATE CLEAN.

FIFTY-FIVE

Blessed Discipline

*Blessed is the man you discipline, O Lord,
the man you teach from your law.*
Psalms 94:12

A basketball coach once said, "Don't worry when I'm yelling at you. Worry when I stop yelling." He was saying that his voice level communicated his concern for the player. So when he quit yelling, he had quit caring.

God's not a yeller, but if you want Him to bless you, expect to be disciplined.

When?

Well, God's kids mess up, sometimes deliberately. And like any good father who knows exactly the right time to discipline, God knows too. He doesn't discipline for spiritual childishness. He expects that. He knows perfection is way off in the future. He disciplines for direct acts of disobedience, things that challenge His authority in ways he knows will eventually hurt you. For example, He will discipline you when you constantly challenge your parents' authority. Why? Because when you do that, you're actually telling God, "You didn't know what you were doing when you gave me these parents. I'm going to do what I want." Bad move.

God isn't "out to get you." He's not waiting for you to step out of line so He can pounce. He's interested in the big picture. From time to time He checks to see if you've taken a wrong turn in your walk, if there are attitudes in your heart that will cause problems for you later on. Then He decides what it's going to take to get you back on the right road.

Which leads to the second question: *How* does He discipline?

As you may have guessed, God is extremely creative—and diligent—when it comes to getting His kids back on the path to life. He works hard to make sure that the walk away from Him is a short one.

His first resort is to use people to get your attention. God will often use your parents, a teacher, a coach, a neighbor, a grandparent, a youth leader, a pastor, even a friend to speak the truth to you. If you listen, you've just taken the easy way.

His second resort is circumstances. If He can't get your attention by truthful words, He'll start *allowing* and *arranging* circumstances in your life. For instance, a student who won't pay attention to the counsel of family and friends when it comes to knuckling down on studies will be allowed to reap the "rewards." Instead of a scholarship at a four-year college, he'll be taking classes at the local community college while working twenty to thirty hours a week to survive.

Instead of being able to marry the type of man who treats her right, a girl who goes against the counsel of those who love her (many voices saying the same thing) will be allowed to see what life is like with the louse she thinks is best for her.

Call it discipline or natural consequences, both will lead to the desired result: coming to your senses and getting back onto the path that leads to *life*.

When God *arranges* circumstances, the discipline will be a little more obvious. An illness or accident will occur—to you or someone you care about—that allows you the time to think and take stock of your chosen path. Perhaps you'll lose your job or get kicked out of your apartment. Whatever it takes to get your attention, God will use it. He's not controlling your choices; He's using circumstances to get you to look around and notice where you're actually going.

And when it comes right down to it, most of us would agree that we actually *want* God to do whatever is necessary to get our attention. No one likes to be disciplined. And it's true, some will want to walk down that road away from God to see what's there. But most would rather have it His way. When you *are* disciplined, the verse that started this devotional makes it clear what happens: you'll be blessed.

MORE REFLECTION:

- "When we are judged by the Lord, we are being disciplined so that we will not be condemned with the world" (1 Corinthians 11:32).
- "My son, do not make light of the Lord's discipline, and do not lose heart when he rebukes you, because the Lord disciplines those he loves, and he punishes everyone he accepts as a son" (Hebrews 12:5-6).

FOR PONDERING FURTHER:

1. Has God ever disciplined you?
2. How about friends you know?

3. Do you want God to discipline you when you head off the path, or would you sometimes rather go your own way without His interference?
4. What is it that makes humans want to head down the wrong path?

LAST THOUGHT:
BE GLAD THAT GOD LOVES YOU ENOUGH TO DISCIPLINE.

FIFTY-SIX

True Beauty

For you created my inmost being;
you knit me together in my mother's womb.
I praise you because I am
fearfully and wonderfully made;
your works are wonderful, I know full well.
Psalms 139:13-14

Everyone has some "imperfection" they don't like:

Thighs that are too big.

Hair that won't stay straight . . . or won't curl.

Baby fat that has turned into adult fat.

A crooked tooth, or two.

Too much arm hair.

Not enough facial hair.

Eyebrows too thick.

Not enough eyebrow hair.

Too tall.

Too short.

Too skinny.

Too chubby.

The sad conclusion many people have come to is that unless they were "blessed" with a pleasant-looking face or near-perfect body, God must not like them. Or worse, He doesn't exist. Or if He does exist, He's got a bad sense of humor and can't be trusted. Every way they look at it, it's God's fault that the Hollywood-induced ideal of beauty passed them by.

As God was looking for a mold to use when He created you, He didn't have to visit a Hollywood set to get a few ideas. He knew exactly what he was doing when he put you together. His goal was not to create a planet filled with models and actors.

Have you heard the phrase, "God don't make no junk!"?

It's true. He knew what he was doing when he knit you together in your mother's womb. The "imperfections" weren't created to make you feel insecure, but to make you unique.

If you know anyone with a good-looking body, then you know that beauty can be a blessing or a curse. The same goes for someone who has a few minor imperfections. There are pluses and minuses that go with each. It's attitude that makes the difference . . . not appearance. Each person has to choose whether to start the comparison game while they're young. They can learn to hate their appearance (and for some, hate God because of it), or learn to accept the body they've been given.

Once you're able to look yourself in the mirror and say, "I'm not perfect, but I accept what I've been given," then you have the freedom to develop what God knows is MOST important: inner character that leads to true beauty.

MORE REFLECTION:

- "For by him all things were created: things in heaven and on earth, visible and invisible, whether thrones or power or

rules or authorities; all things were created by him and for him" (Colossians 1:16).
- "They exchanged the truth of God for a lie, and worshiped and served created things rather than the Creator—who is forever praised. Amen" (Romans 1:25).

FOR PONDERING FURTHER:

1. Name as many of your physical characteristics as you can that you are happy with.
2. What part(s) of your body would you change if you could?
3. What will it take for you to become comfortable with the body God gave you?

LAST THOUGHT:

BE THANKFUL FOR THE BODY YOU'VE BEEN GIVEN, KNOWING THAT IT'S THE INNER CHARACTER THAT GOD IS MOST CONCERNED ABOUT.

FIFTY-SEVEN

The Not-So-Great Pretender

Those who hate the Lord would pretend obedience to him: and their time of punishment would be forever.
Psalms 81:15, NASB

A sports network has a yearly show called "X-Games." In the show they concoct dangerous and wild competitions that usually have the participants going incredible downhill speeds. These guys know that if they fall, they not only lose the competition, but that their legs, arms, and face will have a serious case of road rash.

Many teenagers in churches are playing their own extreme games. It's not as physically dangerous, but the spiritual consequences are far worse than mere road rash. It's the "churchianity" game. The players go to church every week to please their parents, but are never honest enough to admit to them where they are really at with God. Some play the game to keep peace, knowing they can stop when they graduate from high school and leave home. Others are participating unwittingly, not really realizing they're playing the game at all.

It's tough growing up in the church. There's the subtle pressure not to embarrass your parents or be rebellious by staying home from church on Sundays. And friends or the youth pastor have attendance expectations, too. Everyone wants you there so you can learn more about God, Jesus, and the Bible.

But what if you're not interested? What if you don't sense a need for God? What if the Bible is just too boring for you to understand? What if the youth pastor is a little too dorky? What if you don't know the words to the songs they're always singing—or you hate to sing altogether? What if, what if, what if . . .

Do you play-act, pretending you like it? Do you put your foot down and just tell everyone—including your parents—you're not going anymore? Do you show up in body, but act like you're hating every second of it? Do you cause trouble so they get the point that it would be in *everyone's* best interest to leave you home?

How about this novel idea: honesty.

Pretending obedience to God when you really aren't interested isn't the way He wants it (see the above verse). In the long run, it's not the way your parents want it, either. What you owe God, your parents, your friends—yourself—is to be honest about where your heart is toward God. You do that not by throwing an adolescent fit because you have to go to church, but by sitting down with your parents and having an adult conversation, explaining your true beliefs.

Does that mean you'll be able to get out of going to church or youth group if you *are* honest? Not likely. Nor should it mean that. And it's not wise to buck it, either. You know how you feel and what you believe. But if you're *really* honest, you have to admit . . . you *don't* know everything. And if this Christianity stuff is real, it would be a

HUGE mistake to miss out on finally cluing in just because you wanted to watch TV a couple more hours a week.

Whoever cares to know, tell them where you're at (NOTE: but don't use honesty as a way to get attention). But stay involved in church, ask tons of questions, watch closely those who say they truly know Jesus Christ (but cut your Christian friends some slack, realizing they won't be perfect), and don't try to make your parents look stupid by rebelling.

God knows that not everyone will "get it" in high school. And he doesn't want you to pretend you've "got it" when you don't. He much prefers a genuine, seeking heart.

MORE REFLECTION:

- "Now a man named Ananias, together with his wife Sapphira, also sold a piece of property. With his wife's full knowledge he kept back part of the money for himself, but brought the rest and put it at the apostles' feet.

  "Then Peter said, 'Ananias, how is it that Satan has so filled your heart that you have lied to the Holy Spirit and have kept for yourself some of the money you received for the land? Didn't it belong to you before it was sold? And after it was sold, wasn't the money at your disposal? What made you think of doing such a thing? You have not lied to men but to God.'

  "When Ananias heard this, he fell down and died. And great fear seized all who heard what had happened" (Acts 5:1-5).

- "Buy the truth, and do not sell it; get wisdom, discipline, and understanding" (Proverbs 23:23).

FOR PONDERING FURTHER:

1. Have you ever wanted to take a break from church? Why?
2. Do you feel that some of your friends at church are only pretending to like being there?
3. Have you ever thought about being honest about feelings toward God?
4. Are you the type who wants his or her way, or can you admit you don't know everything?

LAST THOUGHT:

BE HONEST WITH YOURSELF AND THOSE WHO LOVE YOU ABOUT WHERE YOU ARE WITH GOD.

FIFTY-EIGHT

The Sin of Divination

Some became fools through their rebellious ways and suffered affliction because of their iniquities.
Psalms 107:17

There's a point somewhere between "willful sin that you're sorry for" and "a lifestyle where God gives you over." That point is rebellion—the consistent, willful departure from what you know to be true. God loves the rebel, even in his or her rebellion, but He sees the fruit of this chosen path and has some strong words for it.

"For rebellion is like the sin of divination, and arrogance like the evil idolatry. Because you have rejected the word of the Lord, he has rejected you as king" (1 Samuel 15:23).

Divination is calling up evil spirits. Have you ever compared rebellion to conjuring up demons? God has. He knows that if you're not listening to and following Him, then you're listening to and following the powers of darkness. No middle ground. It's one or the other.

Rebellion against God and the truth is very serious business. "Cutting your own path," "charting your own course," and "having a mind of your own" aren't simple phrases that describe a personality type.

They're descriptions of someone who wants to live life separated from God's influence. Whether it's low-level rebellion to a parent's authority, or full-blown rebellion to God, the church, and everything related to Christianity, it always starts small. A voice whispers. "You're your own man. Do it your way," or "That's a dumb rule. Do what you want," or "What do God and your parents know? After all, they've never been a teenager in the twenty-first century."

These are voices that can't be heard with the physical ears, but voices so many people are listening to and obeying. Since it's not God's voice, it must be the voice of the evil one. A small seed of rebellion is planted, and it truly is like divination, like calling up demons.

God wants you to think for yourself, and certainly few would want to be thought of as a sheep in the crowd. But in order to escape the potentially devastating consequences of rebellion, you must have a little sheep in you. Go ahead and be a thinker, ask questions, test the truth, but do it with a heart that wants an honest answer—and a heart that wants to follow the Shepherd above all else. This is the type of mind God honors.

Everyone can make the small choices that lead to a rebellion that separates them from God. If someone wants out from under God's covering, He won't force them to stay. But the consequences, according to this verse, are obvious: suffering affliction because of the sinful choices that person makes.

MORE REFLECTION:

- "We know that the law is good if one uses it properly. We also know that law is made not for the righteous but for lawbreakers and rebels, the ungodly and sinful, the unholy and irreligious; for those who kill their fathers or mothers, for murderers, for adulterers and perverts, for slave traders and liars and perjurers—and for whatever else is contrary to the sound doctrine that conforms to the glorious gospel of the blessed God, which he entrusted to me" (1 Timothy 1:8-10).

- "He said, 'Surely they are my people, sons who will not be false to me'; and so he became their Savior. In all their distress he too was distressed, and the angel of his presence saved them. In his love and mercy he redeemed them; he lifted them up and carried them all the days of old. Yet they rebelled and grieved his Holy Spirit. So he turned and became their enemy and he himself fought against them" (Isaiah 63:8-10).

FOR PONDERING FURTHER:

1. Do you think of yourself as rebellious?
2. Did you ever think that rebellion is like calling up demons?
3. Do you agree or disagree with this conclusion?
4. Can rebellion be good?

LAST THOUGHT:

CONSIDER THE SOURCE AND CONSEQUENCES OF REBELLION—AND SEEK TO AVOID BOTH.

FIFTY-NINE

The Hugest Calling of All

May the words of my mouth and the meditation of my heart be pleasing in your sight, O Lord, my Rock and my Redeemer.
Psalms 19:14

If you've meditated (thought about for a little longer than usual) on what is good, most likely your words will reflect it. How do you keep your heart and mind focused on what is good? By reading the Bible (naturally) and other good books, watching good movies and TV shows, and by having friends whose mouths don't sound like they're in a football locker room. Like many things, it comes down to making the right choices on what you ingest in your mind and heart.

If you've thought about what isn't good, again, your mouth will be filled with what you've chosen to focus on. A steady diet of raunchy videos and music, premium channels, R-rated movies, and friends who don't care about what they say fills the heart with words that will eventually be "thrown up."

The psalmist knew that his words and heart were inseparable. He knew that what was in his heart wasn't always good (and he didn't even have 24-7 access to the internet). But he knew whom he wanted to please. That's why he prayed for his heart and his words.

We know that making the constant choice to please the one who lives inside us, the Savior we cannot see ... is a HUGE challenge. But it's the right challenge, isn't it? It's right to set your mind on things that please Him. It's right to want a heart and mind to be pleasing and acceptable in his sight.

MORE REFLECTION:

- "What comes out of a man is what makes him 'unclean.' For from within, out of men's hearts, come evil thoughts, sexual immorality, theft, murder, adultery, greed, malice, deceit, lewdness, envy, slander, arrogance, and folly. All these evils come from inside and make a man 'unclean'" (Mark 7:20-22).
- "Do not let any unwholesome talk come out of your mouths, but only what is helpful for building others up according to their needs, that it may benefit those who listen" (Ephesians 4:29).

FOR PONDERING FURTHER:

1. What does the phrase, "garbage in, garbage out" mean to you?
2. Is it really true? What kind of "garbage" have you put in your heart and mind?

3. Think about your friends or acquaintances who swear a lot or are constantly putting others down. What are their families like? Who do they hang around? What do they watch and listen to?
4. Why do you think God would be displeased with what comes out of your mouth?

LAST THOUGHT:
USE CAUTION WHEN DECIDING WHAT YOU PUT IN YOUR HEART AND MIND.

SIXTY

Off the Chart

*The Lord is gracious and compassionate,
slow to anger and rich in love. The Lord is
good to all; he has compassion on all he has made.*
Psalms 145:8-9

If someone asked you the question, "What is God like?" would you know the answer? What parts of his character would you mention first? Which ones would you leave out?

While you'll never understand all there is to know about God, He definitely doesn't want you to be confused about His character. If you are, then you'll be tempted to keep your distance. One reason the Bible was written (and this book, too) was to tell you that God doesn't want to be distant. He hates it when He's thought of as a concept, a force, or some impersonal being who created humans but now doesn't know what to do with them.

Yes, it's true that God is spirit (which is a tough concept to grasp). But he's much more.

God is love.

He's creative.

He understands perfectly—at all times.

He forgives.

He empowers.

And, as this passage asserts, He's full of compassion.

For all of these qualities—and more—He doesn't just languish at "average" on the chart. He is so far off the chart that it's tough to even imagine how high, deep, and wide these qualities can go.

Humans have limits. For instance, you can push a parent or teacher only so far before their compassion runs out. Not so with God.

If you knew someone at your school with unlimited compassion, would you want to spend time with that person? Would you be drawn to that person—even when you felt you didn't deserve compassion? You should.

Compassion is a character quality that is truly rare in today's world. It's not a hug, an understanding nod of the head, or a knowing smile. It's work.

It's tears.

It's getting your hands dirty for someone else.

When you have true compassion you're an advocate for those who are less fortunate than yourself. A relief worker or doctor who leaves the comfort of her American lifestyle to go to Nigeria to work with babies who have AIDS or adults dying of starvation does so because she has a compassionate heart. She doesn't look down on those less fortunate because they're not Americans. She sees the need and tries to meet it with all of the energy and skill she possesses. Compassion means action.

In the same way, God knows fully that you cannot be perfect. He doesn't blame you because you aren't God. Instead He went into action, showing constant compassion for your condition. How far can

His compassion be pushed? He shows compassion on even the proud and profane.

Whatever positive character quality you ascribe to God, multiply it by 100 and you'll just begin to scratch the surface on the true depth of that quality.

MORE REFLECTION:

- "All of us also lived among them at one time, gratifying the cravings of our sinful nature and following its desires and thoughts. Like the rest, we were by nature objects of wrath. But because of his great love for us, God who is rich in mercy, made us alive with Christ even when we were dead in our transgressions—it is by grace you have been saved" (Ephesians 2:3-5).
- "... the Lord is full of compassion and mercy" (James 5:11b).

FOR PONDERING FURTHER:

1. What positive qualities does God have?
2. When you think about the limits of those qualities, how do you quantify it? Do you compare it to another person, or do you know that it is off the chart?
3. What would you say if someone asked you what God is like?
4. Is there a character quality you've placed on God that is perhaps untrue or unfair?

LAST THOUGHT:

ALLOW YOUR FINITE VIEWS ON GOD'S COMPASSION TO BE SHATTERED BY THE DEPTH OF THAT COMPASSION FOR YOU.

Wrap Up

The key to surviving both the highs and the lows of life is to stay rock-solidly convinced of the character of God. These pages have hit that theme time and again. I hope you've become a bit more established in your faith in the God of the Bible. He can always be trusted, even when life takes you on a wild ride.

I hope you caught something else about God: He's worth loving. His concern for you is both emotional and practical. He'll do anything and everything to show you the extent of His love. But you have to respond to it. My prayer is you'll respond by recognizing the depth of His love for you . . . and loving Him in return. Not just during your teenage years, but throughout your life. It's an adventure you won't want to miss.

SCRIPTURE INDEX

Passage	Chapter	Passage	Chapter
Deuteronomy 31:6	31	Matthew 1:20	23
1 Samuel 15:23	58	Matthew 5:11-12	2
1 Samuel 16:7	36	Matthew 6:13	38
Job 19:25	39	Matthew 7:7-8	26
Psalms 1:1	1	Matthew 10:28-31	35
Psalms 2:6	4	Matthew 11:25-26	53
Psalms 4:4	51	Matthew 18:20	23
Psalms 5:3	8	Matthew 28:20b	31
Psalms 8:3-5	11	Mark 1:35	8
Psalms 9:1	17	Mark 7:20-22	59
Psalms 9:8-9	47	Mark 15:34	3
Psalms 10:1	3	Luke 11:17	52
Psalms 10:4	22	Luke 12:24	11
Psalms 10:13	29	John 8:32	24
Psalms 12:8	38	John 10:14	39
Psalms 14:1-3	24	John 11:35	20
Psalms 15:1-2	3	John 12:47-48	47
Psalms 15:1-5	9	John 15:7	26
Psalms 16:8	45	Acts 4:18-20	17
Psalms 26:11	32	Acts 5:1-5	57
Psalms 17:6	26	Acts 6:3a	34
Psalms 19:7-11	15	Acts 13:38-40	19
Psalms 19:13	28	Acts 14:19-22	46

Psalms 19:14	59	Romans 1:21-24a	50
Psalms 20:7	30	Romans 1:25	56
Psalms 22:1, 24	10	Romans 13:11-14	9
Psalms 22:10	40	Romans 2:4-5	50
Psalms 22:22	53	Romans 5:3-4	21
Psalms 23:4	38, 42	Romans 8:28	10
Psalms 24:1-2	11	Romans 8:38-39	10
Psalms 25:4-5	32	Romans 12:1-2	25
Psalms 25:7	18	Romans 12:18	37
Psalms 25:11	19	Romans 12:21	38
Psalms 25:16-17	46	Romans 13:11-14	9
Psalms 26:2	21	1 Corinthians 1:8-9	44
Psalms 27:1	35	1 Corinthians 3:11-15	29
Psalms 27:4	5	1 Corinthians 11:32	56
Psalms 27:10	31	1 Corinthians 13:12	24
Psalms 30:5b	20	1 Corinthians 15:33	1
Psalms 31:7	16	1 Corinthians 10:13	28
Psalms 31:8	13	2 Corinthians 3:2-3	34
Psalms 32:1-2	54	2 Corinthians 4:4	13
Psalms 33:13-15	36	2 Corinthians 5:1-5	5
Psalms 34:4	35	2 Corinthians 5:17, 20	36
Psalms 34:12-14	37	2 Corinthians 6:14	1
Psalms 34:14	38	2 Corinthians 9:6-8	12
Psalms 34:18-19	43	2 Corinthians 11:14	23
Psalms 37:4	44	2 Corinthians 11:23-28	46
Psalms 37:7-9	26	Galatians 2:20	4

Psalms 37:21	12	Ephesians 2:3-5	60
Psalms 37:37	37	Ephesians 3:16-17a	4
Psalms 39:4	7	Ephesians 4:29	59
Psalms 40:10	53	Ephesians 5:15-16	38
Psalms 42:1-2	49	Ephesians 6:18	45
Psalms 46:1-3	43	Philippians 3:18-20a	41
Psalms 49:10	14	Philippians 3:20-21	5
Psalms 49:16-17	27	Philippians 4:4	20
Psalms 52:17	25	Philippians 4:8	6
Psalms 55:22	33	Colossians 1:16	56
Psalms 58:11	29	Colossians 2:13-14	19
Psalms 68:19-20	43	Colossians 2:18	23
Psalms 69:6	34	Colossians 3:103	6
Psalms 77:11-12	48	Colossians 4:2	52
Psalms 78:37-39	7	1 Thessalonians 5:16	2
Psalms 81:9	30	1 Thessalonians 5:17	45
Psalms 81:12	50	1 Thessalonians 5:22	38
Psalms 81:15	57	1 Timothy 1:8-10	58
Psalms 84:10	39	1 Timothy 6:7	27
Psalms 86:11	52	2 Timothy 2:22	18
Psalms 86:12-13	17	2 Timothy 4:16-18a	46
Psalms 90:12	42	Hebrews 1:4-5	23
Psalms 91:11-12	23	Hebrews 2:14-15, 17-18	16
Psalms 94:12	55	Hebrews 4:12	15
Psalms 97:10	38	Hebrews 4:15-16	16
Psalms 101:3	6	Hebrews 4:16	33
Psalms 103:13-18	7	Hebrews 10:5-7, 10	25
Psalms 107:17	58	Hebrews 10:23	44

Psalms 115:1	41	Hebrews 12:5-6	55
Psalms 118:24	2, 42	Hebrews 13:2	23
Psalms 119:105	49	Hebrews 13:6	2
Psalms 119:11, 15-16	49	James 1:12	21
Psalms 119:37	6	James 1:19-20	51
Psalms 119:115	1	James 5:11b	60
Psalms 130:5-6	8	1 Peter 1:22-25	15
Psalms 139:13-14	56	1 Peter 5:5-6	18
Psalms 141:4	38	1 Peter 5:7	33
Psalms 145:8-9	60	2 Peter 2:9	28
Proverbs 9:9	14	1 John 1:9	54
Proverbs 14:6-8	14	1 John 2:16-17	22
Proverbs 16:18	22	1 John 2:19	38
Proverbs 16:33	41	1 John 4:4	13
Proverbs 16:33	41	1 John 5:11-12	30
Proverbs 22:24-25	51	1 John 5:19	38
Proverbs 23:23	57		
Ecclesiastes 7:14	48		
Ecclesiastes 12:1	48		

ABOUT THE AUTHOR

Greg Johnson is the Founder and President of WordServe Literary Group and FaithHappenings.com. He has been a literary agent for 21 years, and has personally represented more than 2,300 books.

Before working with authors, Greg wrote 23 non-fiction books and more than 200 magazine articles. He worked for five years as founding editor for "Breakaway" magazine, and spent ten years working full time with youth in the Pacific Northwest.

Greg is married to Becky, who works closely with him in evaluating authors and their manuscripts. Together they have six adult children, along with seven grandchildren. They make their home in Highlands Ranch, Colorado.

Greg is the author of several other books in print, including:
- *101 Family Meal-Time Devotions*
- *10 Reasons to Stay Christian in High School*
- *The 25 Days of Christmas: Family Readings and Scriptures for the Advent Season*
- *If I Could Ask God Just One Question*

ABOUT THE PUBLISHER

FH Publishers is a division of FaithHappenings.com

FaithHappenings.com is the premier, first-of-its kind, online Christian resource that contains an array of valuable local and national faith-based information all in one place. Our mission is "to inform, enrich, inspire and mobilize Christians and churches while enhancing the unity of the local Christian community so they can better serve the needs of the people around them." FaithHappenings.com will be the primary i-Phone, Droid App/Site and website that people with a traditional Trinitarian theology will turn to for national and local information to impact virtually every area of life.

The vision of FaithHappenings.com is to build the vibrancy of the local church with a true "one-stop-resource" of information and events that will enrich the soul, marriage, family, and church life for people of faith. We want people to be touched by God's Kingdom, so they can touch others FOR the Kingdom.

To learn more, visit www.faithhappenings.com.

www.ingramcontent.com/pod-product-compliance
Lightning Source LLC
Chambersburg PA
CBHW031640040426
42453CB00006B/170